Animal Angels

Animal Angels

True Tales of Creatures
That Changed and Enriched People's Lives

By
Charlene R. Johnson
and
Michael Rebel

New Horizon Press
Far Hills, New Jersey

Charlene R. Johnson and Michael Rebel
        Animal Angels: True Tales of Creatures That Changed and Enriched People's Lives

Cover Design: Michael Stromberg, The Great American Art Company
Interior Design: Susan M. Sanderson

Library of Congress Control Number: 2003105758
ISBN: 0-88282-234-9
New Horizon Press

Manufactured in the U.S.A.

2007   2006   2005   2004   2003   /   5   4   3   2   1

Charlene's Dedication

I wish to dedicate this book to my parents. They were my first teachers, my first loves. My father opened the door to the world of spirituality even before I can remember; my mother has always been there with her unconditional love. Both gifts are beyond measure.

Michael's Dedication

This work has been directly affected by many people, quite literally, by all those that have come through my life. Those who were extraordinary influences included my parents, who had the courage and faith in God's care to allow me to roam unencumbered on this earth since I was three years old. Then there have been my mentors: Etna Crowder in my high school years; Michael and Linda O'Connor challenged and trusted me in my college years; Elisabeth Pringle exposed me to the world of psychology and gave me a solid theoretical beginning. Her trust was my springboard into the profession. I thank Barbara Gulesserian for her support while we learned and Peggy Keene for convincing me that my natural instincts were worth teaching and writing about.

I also prosper in the same support that all humans share on this planet, mother earth for her life support, God for the divine plan, humanity for its co-travelers and loved ones, the trees for air to breathe and the animals for their part in the divine plan.

Contents

Acknowledgments

Michael and I both have many thanks to offer in the creation of this book. Not by order of importance, but by order of specificity, we begin our list. The first angels we want to thank are also authors. We wish to thank Ted Andrews for writing his most excellent books, *Animal-Speak* and *Animal-Wise*. Although both Michael and I have studied animals and things Native American and understand much of this material already, no one can know everything and these two books have truly become bibles in our lives and in the Natural Awakenings Programs workshops. To be able to draw on this wealth of knowledge at any time, to have the words at our fingertips so that we and the clients can actually find words which strike home, provides an invaluable tool.

The other similar influence, which is both a book and a deck of cards, is the excellent *Medicine Cards: The Discovery of Power Through the Ways of Animals* by Jamie Sams and David Carson. Not a workshop goes by that people don't draw their cards for the day or the issue. When it is not possible to be out of doors or we are tight on time and therefore don't have an opportunity for the real animal to come to us, it is wonderful to have this tool to draw upon. The drawing of these cards never fails to stimulate ah-hahs, conversation and deeper insights.

The writing of this book would have been far more difficult without these resources, both as tools and as further proof of the premises we present in this book.

Michael has issued thanks of his own, and I wish to specifically thank three of the same people he mentioned, Elisabeth Pringle, Peggy Keene, Barbara Gulesserian as angels in my life also. All four (including Michael) came into my life at a time when I was desperately seeking assistance with my own life struggles. There was recognition from the beginning, and all five of us have become close friends. Natural

Awakenings was just getting started; the concept of animal angels had just been born and I was privileged to be a part of it as it has evolved and grown into successful workshops, a wonderful collection of stories and finally this book.

I wish to thank Michael for recognizing a potential partner, friend and co-worker in me. I believe his therapeutic intuition is inspired and I am very proud to be associated with him. We have shared much over the years and I feel he is as close a friend as I have ever had. He has certainly been an angel in my life.

I also wish to thank the intimate relationships in my life which have, in the past, seemed to be the source of so much pain, but in fact also caused the most growth in understanding and love. You know who you are; you are all still very much loved.

Michael and I both certainly want to thank all of the wonderful people who were willing to bare their souls, rub the scabs of past pain and share with us and all of you reading this book their often hard-to-believe stories. Believe them. They are all real. This book would not have been possible without every one of them.

We could also thank the animals who are part of this book. But animals, unlike people, do not worry about their missions in life, and therefore would probably not need thanks. They do not worry about whether they do right or wrong, or whether they are good or bad animals. They do what they are created to do and then they go. We can learn a lot from the animal world. So perhaps it would be more appropriate to thank God for creation, this glorious creation which includes the animals, plants and minerals, all of which are part of our existence.

Lastly, we want to thank you for picking up this book and being open enough to explore the concept of animal angels.

This book is about acceptance. By the end, we hope you understand what we mean. So much of the pain in life is because we fight so hard. It is only when we awaken and realize this that we can receive the grace for which we are all so hungry. Learning to accept is one of our hardest lessons, which are the lessons the animals teach so well.

Much love to you all, Charlene R. Johnson

chapter one

Animal Angels

Holy Mother Earth
the trees and all nature
are witnesses of your thoughts and deeds
—*saying of the Winnebago Tribe*

Charlene said that she went crazy in 1996. Though some call it entering the dark night of the soul, she didn't know exactly what was wrong with her, what to call it or even what do do about it.

"These things I know," Charlene said. "I was suffering post partum blues from the completion of an eight-year-long book project which I had felt was spiritually inspired. But that book was stagnating in my computer, unsold, and had generated a sense of disconnection. I was desperately in love with a man who hadn't been able to tell me that he loved me in seven years of living together. I was starving for love, and starving for a spiritual life, starving for meaning in my world. At the time I couldn't put all that into words. Life had lost its meaning and when I looked around I couldn't see that I was doing anything that mattered at all. I felt like I was dying.

"For a year I floundered. I hurt people who loved me and confused my friends. Finally, in complete desperation, I launched myself like an unguided missile into the dark unknown. I left the best man I'd ever been with or loved. I left my job and the most stable home I'd ever had. I moved, penniless, into the woods, where I lived in a woodshed for the next ten months. My family thought I'd gone nuts and my friends dwindled in number, but I suspected that I had begun the search for my soul.

"I buried myself in my tiny, dark shed in the woods, sorting through crushing guilt, wild emotions and thoughts that were far from clear. Walking had always been my favorite exercise but it became therapeutic for me. Every day, I walked from my little haven in the trees onto dirt roads that wound through the woods and eventually onto a paved road that through a peaceful residential area and back again. Every day I walked past several backwoods mobile homes and every day I saw a pit bull tied to a tree outside one of them. He roared and spat and lunged against his rope each time he saw me passing by. I was sure that one day he would break that flimsy rope and hurt somebody or something.

"On this particular day as I walked past, I felt the usual surge of anger at people who keep dogs tied up and apparently forget that these animals need exercise, attention, love and something to do. How could you blame the dog for being angry at circumstances that left him tied on a short rope to a tree where boredom must have killed his spirit every day and every night of his life?

"I walked on, engulfed in a turmoil of emotions caused by my own choking rope of fear, fallen expectations and shame. Like the pit bull, I was frustrated with the circumstances of my life. My spirit was near death from trying to fit into society's rules and from holding expectations that had never been fulfilled. Like the pit bull, I had been lunging against my ropes and boundaries, snarling with rage and frustration. Finally, I had snapped the rope. The sudden snap threw me flat on my face and here I was, floundering in the dirt and not sure what to attack. Without those limitations, however, I felt rudderless. Without any sort of guidance or knowledge of where my next steps should take me, I had to walk along, using instinct as my guide. I realized that I had no self-confidence whatsoever.

"As a youngster, I was intensely shy, unable to talk or interact with others my own age. I had only animals and nature for friends. I grew up next to a Shoshone-Bannock reservation in Idaho. My father, a minister, often took me along with him on his trips to the reservation. This was an era when Native Americans experienced prejudice and many difficulties. In the little town where I lived, I watched white men force native women with papooses on their backs off the sidewalks and into the streets. As young as I was, I knew that something was wrong with that picture.

"I saw the squalor, the hovels and the extreme poverty of the people who lived on the reservation. But I also saw a proud people, silent to us, the whites, but watchful. Because of my shyness I rarely spoke to them. But today, I know that they knew who I was. When the men rode their Indian ponies up to the tiny house where they would meet with my father, they would often walk to me with their ponies' rope and toss it near me, around a tree or a hitching post and walk into the house without a word. Until they came back out, I sat or stood near the pony, scratching its neck and wondering at the tiny leather bags tied high up under the mane. Even then, I felt the horses were special. I told my parents that when I grew up, I wanted to be an Indian and ride a horse. Until I went to college my only loves were animals, nature, Native American culture and writing.

"As an adult, two dreams came true. I worked professionally in the thoroughbred horse industry and became a turf writer, a journalist covering the thoroughbred industry. Working with horses *and* writing was a dream job for many years, but after a while, the politics of that industry did not match my own belief system so I used the publishing of my first book, *Florida Thoroughbred* as my swan song and began the search for a new career.

"Other parts of me were not happy as well. The traditional church of my youth didn't seem to accept all people and didn't show much love of the earth or believe animals went to heaven. I didn't even know if I believed it, but I didn't want spiritual doors closed on the things none of us can completely understand in this existence. As I grew older, I began exploring my lifetime love of all things Native American and began seriously studying the cultures and beliefs.

"In 1995, when, as the proverb goes, the student was ready, the teacher appeared. Although my instructor lived a Native American style life, he did not limit himself, or me, to that. He had traveled the world all his life, living with so-called primitive cultures from Peru to Tibet and his brand of spirituality encompassed everything. I inhaled what he taught. I heard things that I'd never heard any human say, yet they touched a deep chord of remembering inside me. Finally, his teachings were part of what launched me into the emotional and spiritual revival I was experiencing. As I exited the woods and stepped out onto the paved road that day, I was thinking that I wasn't sure if my teacher was a blessing or a curse.

"I looked up from my musings to see an unlikely pair of dogs trotting toward me, a long-legged, black Labrador retriever and a small Jack Russell terrier whose little legs seemed to blur as he trotted twenty to one to keep pace with the lab. My heart lurched at the sight. I had left my own Jack Russell, with my mate when I left. The woods, with no fenced yard and a woodshed barely big enough for me was no place for an energetic, spoiled house pet. It hurt to leave him almost as much as it had hurt to leave my mate.

"The two dogs trotted straight toward me as I walked on. When they came abreast of me, as if on cue, they swung about to accompany me. As they followed, I began to worry that I was taking them away from their home, wherever that was, and that if they were hit by a car, it would be my fault. I tried to shoo them away, but neither would leave. They didn't pay me much attention; they simply refused to leave me.

"We completed the loop of the residential area together and as I headed back toward the woods, I kept hoping they would swing off to whatever house they lived in. I didn't want them following me into the woods where they might get lost. We were nearing my dirt road when a car slowly drove by and someone leaned out a window, whistling at the dogs. The car stopped. I breathed a sigh of relief as both dogs ran to the car. The car door opened, someone called, and the

Jack Russell leaped happily inside. The door slammed shut and the car drove on, leaving the lab still standing there, his tail wagging as he watched the car drive away. It was as if they'd never seen the big black dog. When the car disappeared around a bend, the lab swung around and trotted back to my side as if to say, 'Where to now, partner?'

"Again I tried to chase him away and again he simply ignored me. When he swung aside to pursue an interesting smell at the side of the road, I tried to outwalk him. Always, though, he came gamboling back up as if I would surely be happy to see him. I worried that I was leading him farther and farther from his home. Finally, when we came to a fork in the road, he loped on ahead down the wrong fork. I nearly ran around the bend. When I looked over my shoulder, it seemed I'd finally lost him. I relaxed and resumed my usual pace. Almost instantly, I fell back into my mournful reveries, zoning out everything else around me.

"Sudden, ferocious snarling shocked me back to where I was. I looked up to see the pit bull lunging at his chain, not one hundred yards from me. My teacher had taught me that we possess all the protection we need, always. Only our fears allow us to be harmed. I believed in that theory, in my head. But I'd never been tested. Did I believe it enough? In my heart?

"Even as the prophetic question arose in my mind, the dog snapped the rope, tumbled head over heels and was instantly on his feet racing for me, low, deadly and snarling. I froze, facing him, knowing that to run would be certain death.

"Suddenly, from nowhere the black lab leaped in front of me and stood stock-still, head up, ears alert, facing the charging pit bull. I stood equally still just inches behind him. The pit bull's snarling rumbled to a growl; his muscular, deadly stride faltered. The lab didn't move a hair or make a sound. The pit bull stumbled and slowed, his flattened ears drooped and, as suddenly as it began, his attack fell apart. He slid off to the side, hesitated, then turned and slunk back to the tree, glancing over his shoulder only once.

"I turned to walk down the road, watching both dogs over my shoulder, petrified that they would get into a fight. I feared that one or both would be injured and I would be blamed. The lab remained where he was, like a black statue on guard until I rounded a bend in the road. Then my knees buckled. Shaking, I took a breath and stumbled on. The lab trotted up gaily from behind me, cast a happy, tongue-lolling grin my way, then dashed into the woods and out of my life forever.

"As he disappeared, I knew that lab was an angel. It occurred to me that he'd probably been called off on a new mission, so suddenly did he take his leave. He had been sent to this time and place for me. I'd been walking those woods for a couple of months and had never seen him before. In ten months of living there and walking every day, I never saw him again. I knew I'd been sent a gift.

"But it was not until I sat down to write this story that I realized, I had played my part in protecting myself as well. By believing that such things as facing down a charging pit bull were possible and by not setting up expectations of where that protection would come from or what it would look like, I had kept the door open to any possibility. An animal angel had dropped down in front of me. But he had not come to rescue me. I did not need to be rescued from a pit bull. I needed to believe in myself. I needed to believe in my connection to the divine."

Following her episode with the dogs, Charlene realized that she needed to seek professional help for her emotional unrest. A close friend pointed her in the direction of a therapist in Ocala, Florida, who turned out to be the next angel on her journey. After several sessions in which the therapist managed to stabilize and calm Charlene—by then, she was a living, breathing basket case—the therapist called her one night, and exclaimed excitedly, "Charlene, I think I have just the workshop for you! It is run by friends of mine who are very good therapists. They've started holding workshops for people like you who are passionate about nature. I really think these are your kind of people. He's a nature boy and she's a medicine woman!" When she read Charlene the description of the workshop, goose bumps covered Charlene's arms. She knew her therapist was right—this was for her! Money or not, somehow, she had to get to that workshop.

Charlene arrived on Michael's welcoming doorstep with the feeling that this was her last hope. Group therapy and talking about herself in a circle of strangers was the last thing in the world she ever dreamed was possible. It was a sign of how desperate she'd become. Never would Charlene have believed that she could stretch that far.

"Charlene said, "The therapist who sent me told me that Michael looked like a teddy bear and indeed, it seemed to be a teddy bear opening the door to me. Rotund, bearded and dimpled, he instantly put my quaking heart and lurching stomach to rest—at least for the moment. I would soon find out that although he exudes caring, Michael also knows how to go right to the heart of a matter; his therapeutic intuition is uncanny."

After hearing the story of the black lab and the attacking pit bull, Michael quickly pointed out that not only was Charlene's black lab an angel in her life, but it also represented her own dark side, the part of her hardest to see or accept, the part of her that could tear something else apart for self protection. It was a concept she had never come close to recognizing. The idea was something tough to swallow…but never had anything felt so right.

Thus began not only a therapeutic relationship that helped Charlene on the long road to healing, awakening and growing, but also a relationship which grew into a deep and mutually beneficial friendship. Charlene needed a healer. Michael needed a writer. They both, like everyone, needed good friends.

The idea of a book called *Animal Angels* was originally conceived by Michael Rebel. A couple of years before he met Charlene, he realized that he continually heard stories about animals that had major impacts on his clients, although the clients didn't always recognize what had happened until he pointed it out. His recognition of what the animals meant came from his own understanding of nature.

"In some ways, I was like the boy who was raised by the wolves," he explained. "I had a home, but I was more connected to the outdoors than I was to the house or my family. I learned everything from the animals. When I was young I received very little nurturing at home. I did not have what some would call a happy childhood, but I was full of wonder at the world I lived in. I was outdoors all the time."

Michael was born and raised in the countryside of central Florida. By the time he was three, he was traipsing alone through the

woods and citrus orchards around his home. More than once his frantic mother called his father home from his work as a history and social
sciences schoolteacher to track Michael down and bring him home. "If
they'd just waited, I'd have come home by dark," Michael said. "I was
never lost." Michael's best friend and constant companion was a dog
named Patty.

From the beginning, Michael knew things about nature that he
could not explain. He would tell his mother, a science teacher, things
about animals and plants that she'd never heard. When she asked him
how he knew, he would shrug and say, "I just know." She began looking his statements up in her science books. "She told me that I freaked
her out," Michael said. "I was always right and she couldn't figure out
how I could know."

At first, he didn't understand that he was different. He assumed
everybody knew the things he knew. But eventually his mother's fear
and anxiety got through to him and he learned to keep his mouth shut.
As he grew into adulthood he was labeled eccentric and his self-confidence collapsed.

He checked into American society in the usual fashion, married and raised a family. He worked as a commercial fisherman, a land-
scaper and an orange grove worker. It was when his second marriage
fell apart that he, like so many of his future clients, realized he had no
clue how to keep a relationship together. He also became aware that he
was terribly unhappy. He went looking for help and found a therapist
in Leesburg, Florida named Elisabeth Pringle, Psy.D. She was the first
recognized angel in Michael's life. With her, Michael began peeling the
layers from his own psychological onion, diving into his dark side and
looking at the less than pretty parts of his own psyche.

In the process, he learned not only about his problems, but also
about his talents. Michael found that he had a real ability to help others. He went back to school and became a licensed mental health counselor, later adding training in Gestalt therapy, hypnotherapy and emotional release therapies. Before long, he began realizing that his unique
connection to nature had value in his work with troubled individuals.
He was able to integrate his knowledge of nature and its natural order
into his therapeutic work.

After several years of practicing as a therapist, Michael met a talented therapist who soon became his partner. While they were together, his partner also became interested in Native American ceremonies and traditions. She began to study them, finding beliefs and values that she had been unable to find elsewhere. Michael watched over her shoulder, and realized that much of what he already knew and believed was in fact traditional Native American belief.

Michael and his partner attended a Native American workshop together. As part of the weekend activities they were sent off into the woods to observe animals and come back with the story of one that had impacted them in some way.

"In typical fashion," Michael said, laughing, "I wanted to come back from my walk with the best animal possible, a cougar or a wolf or something powerful. Well, when we started sharing our stories of the different animals people saw, one person said a rabbit and the leader exclaimed, 'A rabbit! Powerful medicine! It knows how to be soft and cuddly and just when to hide in order to be safe.' Then another person said a mouse and the leader said, 'A mouse! Powerful medicine! They are masters at getting into small places and finding food when everyone else is starving. They know just how much food they need to put away for the winter.' As we went on, I realized that all animals are powerful medicine! I'd been watching animals all my life. I was aware of the importance of all of them in terms of the food chain and the overall circle of life, but I was as biased as most people are, thinking of some creatures as great animals and others as insignificant. I'd never made the connection to how important *all* animals are. That was sort of the building block for my starting to pay attention."

At that point, it was like popcorn popping. Suddenly insights and revelations leapt into his consciousness that would change the way he conducted therapy forever. "I started seeing animal totems in people," Michael went on. "For instance, I clearly saw a woman with a skunk totem. By pointing out to her that skunk is powerful medicine and an effective way of maintaining distance, and that she might want to be more aware of it so that she could choose when to put it out and when not, it changed her life. It's a very non-threatening way of addressing people's defenses or issues. You can't always tell people the kind of animal you see as their medicine. Some would be offended, but it's given me a very powerful tool in my therapeutic work.

"Then, I was working one day and realized a new definition of what an angel is. An angel is anything, any manifest energy sent by the universe to teach us or to carry us to newer heights of understanding and acceptance. When I recognized that, I had a renewed sense of faith, of correctness, a renewed connection to God. It was like an angel had passed through my life right at that moment, granting me the ability to see that I was an angel in other people's lives. Then I thought, *Why would God restrict the angel to human form?* And it hit me, *Wow, animal angels!*

"As soon as I had the concept, I started seeing it all around me. I was able to recall instances from the past that fit into the pattern as well. It's kind of like the way you never see a certain kind of car until you buy one, then you see it everywhere. I became acutely aware of this phenomenon. I even tested it. I wanted to be sure that this was real.

"I started incorporating it into my work, using it as a therapeutic tool, an exploratory tool. If someone comes in and says that he or she is stuck, or says 'I don't know what's going on with me,' I ask them 'What kind of animals are you seeing?' Or I'll ask the person to be aware of when animals approach him or her. It frequently breaks up the logjam inside of the individual, and the person is often able to approach their problems from totally different perspectives."

Michael himself was a participant in a therapists' workshop one weekend when he decided to introduce the concept of animal angels as an idea, to see what other professionals thought of it. He said, "A woman came up to me and said she needed to talk to me. She said she had a client who had the strangest thing happen to him. He was jogging through Central Park in New York City one day and an owl swooped down and attacked him, actually raked his head with its talons and left him bleeding. She asked me what I thought that meant.

"I told her that I believed animals could see energies, so they recognize certain kinds of energy. Perhaps the owl saw this guy as a mouse; he'd kind of shape-shifted and taken on the magnetic field of a mouse. I told her I expected this guy had probably adopted some of the characteristics of a mouse, was very mild, secretive, might hide things and try not to be noticed in order to survive. She was astonished. She said I'd described him perfectly. She was able to go back and help the man turn his life around."

It was when Michael heard another therapist's powerful animal story (we'll discuss Marjorie and the sparrow in another chapter) during a workshop for therapists that the idea of a book first came to him. "When I was driving home I was thinking about the power of that story. When she told her story, the entire group was impacted by it. I thought, *This has value.* That's when the idea of the book came to me. It would be cool to pass it on and open up people's awareness of the concept of animal angels."

Today, Michael's practice includes a long-time dream of his, workshops held in nature, incorporating the natural energy of the universe into therapeutic sessions. In 1996, after several experimental formats, the Natural Awakenings Programs were born and proved themselves an instant success.

"The idea of putting people into nature who don't often get that chance and encouraging them to interact with the earth, trees and animals as part of their therapy is extremely effective," Michael said. "It brings them back to God."

The concept of Animal Angels has been a part of the workshops from the beginning. Michael and his assistants rely on several theories dealing with animal medicine. Most people who come to the workshops are able to accept the idea instantly. Animals have universal appeal. After even a very short time at one of Michael's workshops, people begin to have a feeling for what this animal or that bird means, to such a degree that if a bird flies up to the window, everyone knows who it is for and what its message is.

"What I try to teach people is, once you really believe in this concept and begin to experiment with and hypothesize about it, you just start looking. When you see an animal, you stop and think, 'What was I pondering, what was my question at this moment?' Sometimes it's just about what it means in this moment no matter what I'm thinking, but you'll know the difference.

"I've come up with a metaphor of how it feels in my life," Michael explained. "I have a sense of God sitting up there in the clouds, writing messages on paper airplanes and sailing them down in front of us. That little paper airplane flies into your life and it's got a message, a life message, a moment message or a spiritual message that's symbolized by the exact animal that came to you and has symbolized certain things for mankind from the time man began looking to the gods for answers.

"Now in my life, every time I get one of those little airplanes, I immediately pay attention. It really works as a foundation for me. God isn't dead; the universe isn't some concrete, inert, particulate mass rolling in space. There's something going on, just as there is in your body. Your brain knows what your muscles need and sends a message down to them, or it tells your left foot to start walking forward because of where you're standing, or knows just how high to lift your footsteps. The universe is like our physical bodies with all these messages shooting around; everything is informing everything else, everything is communicating with everything else.

"My concept of angels is that they are messengers; they come to teach us philosophically and spiritually. Humans are angels too, some of us bring messages to each other. The trees and the rocks can be angels as well. But we're focusing on animals because we're so acutely attuned to them in our culture. We're fascinated with them. Trees behave so differently to us. They have an electromagnetic frequency that is so far from ours that most of us don't understand, can't relate. We can't absorb what they project as easily as we can animals."

Although workshops and therapists are excellent tools, it is also important to recognize that the animal angel who comes to you has come to *you*, and only *you* know its real meaning. "It's a little like free association," Michael said. "Your first thought is probably the most accurate one. It comes in an instant when the subconscious can blurt out what it knows without being contaminated by the conscious thought."

This book is a collection of stories about animal angels. Not just animals that rescue people from attacking dogs or burning buildings, but animals that have impacted people to such a degree that they've changed their lives. Some of the animals are domestic, some are wild; sometimes the people knew the animals, sometimes the animals show up and deliver their message and then, like Charlene's black lab, disappear forever. They are all different and they are all wonderful. Most of the names of the people have been changed for reasons of privacy, but they are all as real as their animal angels are.

Some find a few of these stories difficult to believe or accept. It will depend upon your own belief systems. We are not attempting to change your convictions or convince you to accept ours. We offer true stories, some of which have supernatural elements, and suggest simply that you do not let the concept offend you. Retain an open mind. We offer what we have learned as a hypothesis. Know that we're not trying to establish any rules that you have to live by nor are we advocating a specific belief system. In fact, when we use the word God or universe, please translate that into whatever creed works best for you, whatever you call your Higher Power.

Michael gives this a supporting suggestion. "I heard the author of *Spontaneous Healing*, Andrew Weil, say that there is no one way of healing everyone, there is only one way that will heal any individual. So whenever what you're doing isn't working, experiment with something else."

Most of all, we hope that you enjoy these wonderful stories and perhaps, while reading, these special animals and people will help you to remember or see your own animal angels. We are sure from our own experiences that they are there to find.

chapter two

Fear

And I think over again my small adventures,
When with a shore wind I drifted out in my kayak,
And thought I was in danger.
My fears, those I thought so big
For all the vital things I had to get and to reach.
And yet, there is only one great thing,
The only thing
To live to see in huts and on journeys
The great day that dawns
And the light that fills the world.
—*Eskimo Song*

"Fear is the single biggest issue we deal with in therapy," Michael said. "Fear is the enemy; it's what suppresses love. It's what gets in the way of accepting things, feeling good, living our lives as fully and happily as we were meant to live them."

Fear alone, however, isn't negative. Fear warns us of real danger. It's a system of protection and letting us know whether some thing, person or place, is hostile or not.

"The way fear becomes negative," Michael explained, "is when it's unwarranted fear, fear that's linked to some past incident in which one was traumatized. Instead of evaluating the present situation and coming up with a real definition of threat or not, the person has an automatic set of behaviors. He or she is really responding to the past rather than the present. That's the kind of fear-based behavior that can look irrational to another person."

Any behavior generated by fear without regard to the present truth is behavior we can choose to change. Sometimes we just need a little help, as an elderly woman named Kaki did. An animal angel improved her life forever.

Kaki and Thorne

Barb and her husband Steve are both talented artists, living on several acres of unkempt farmland in central Florida. They have always been surrounded by dogs, turkeys and various other creatures that need a home or provide a service.

Thorne was Barb and Steve's year-and-a-half-old Rottweiler. According to Barb, he was an American Rottweiler, rather than German, which meant that he was a little smaller and friendlier-looking. "He never looked like a threatening Rottweiler," Barb said. "Of course, that was also because he had all his bits and pieces. He never had his tail docked or his ears trimmed so he didn't look like a 'normal' Rotty."

Thorne endeared himself to all who met him. His gentleness and pure, sweet love were written all over his square black and brown face and in his large, liquid eyes. He was still very much like a puppy, with gangly legs and stocky body.

Barb's mother, Gertrud, lived on the sixth floor of a retirement home in Indiana, just outside of Indianapolis. Everything in this home was self-contained; it was inhabited strictly by retired people, no pets allowed. But Gertrud was very much her daughter's mother and aware of the healing properties of animals. "She knew there were a lot of people who missed having dogs and pets around," Barb explained. "And she knew that interaction with animals lowers blood pressure and does all kinds of good, healthy things for people."

Gertrud had many friends in the home who she felt would benefit from a visit by the huge, gentle dog, so she obtained permission from the powers-that-be in the retirement home, and Barb was allowed to bring Thorne on a visit after assuring them of the dog's gentleness and his excellent training. Barb and Steve are true animal people. They know the exact balance of love and discipline that is necessary to properly raise animals who must live with people.

"Thorne is so well-mannered and laid back," Barb said. "He's one of those dogs that wouldn't dream of offending anyone. When we first got to Mom's retirement community, the security people came to check him out and, of course, they fell in love with him too. They said it was okay and we walked Thorne into the courtyard. People were sitting outside waiting for the bus, enjoying the air or waiting for family. Thorne would stop at each person who wanted to pet him and stand still so they could have the opportunity."

Thorne was on a leash at Barb's side, but by leaning towards the people and granting them a look, he conveyed to her which people wanted to pet him. She allowed him to approach those people to accept their scratches and pets on his massive head. But when he sensed either fear or no desire to be near him, he padded softly by, his great head turned in another direction.

The same thing happened when they entered the building and traveled down the halls. People came up to pet him and he allowed it, leaning forward to receive their loving as if he knew how badly they needed to shower love on him. When they walked into the elevator to go to the sixth floor, he became sixty pounds of limp muscle quivering against Barb's leg. "He didn't know what that moving box was about!" she said. "When he gets scared, he just goes limp."

To Thorne's relief, they made it safely to Gertrud's apartment, where he quickly forgot his own fear in favor of doing his job. Gertrud had already called in a number of her friends. "I took him off his leash and let him do whatever he thought proper," Barb said. "He went to each person in turn. They were all so excited, and of course, everyone fell in love with him. Then Mom called her friend Kaki who lived on the fourth floor." Kaki was the main reason Gertrud had arranged this whole event in the first place.

Kaki had agoraphobia, which is a fear of leaving one's home. She had not been out of her own tiny apartment in two years. Anything she needed, she ordered in. Anytime someone wanted to see her, he or she had to go to her apartment to visit. She loved animals and desperately wanted to have a pet, but the management of the home would not even allow her a bird.

"Mom knew Kaki loved animals," Barb said, "particularly big dogs. So she called her up and told her that Thorne was in her apartment, but he was afraid of elevators. Kaki would have to come up to her apartment to see him."

Kaki tried to figure out another way. Couldn't they walk him down the steps? Couldn't they stop on their way out? Couldn't they... Cheerfully, Gertrud told her that there were too many other people who were still coming to visit Thorne in her apartment. She said that she hoped Kaki could make it up to her place before he had to go home, then hung up.

Kaki was desperate to pet that dog. Finally, full of fear, she left her apartment for the first time since she'd moved in and traveled up two flights of stairs and arrived, out of breath and white as a sheet, at Gertrud's door. "She was scared to death, trembling and panting," Barb said.

Kaki entered the apartment and collapsed onto the floor. Thorne left the person he was with and went straight to her. He lay down in front of her and put his huge head in her lap, staring up at her with big, dark eyes. She fell forward, wrapping her arms around him. "I'm sure she petted him for a good forty-five minutes," Barb said. "You could almost see the healing going on there. Occasionally he'd get up to go see someone else, but he always came back to her. He definitely singled her out and she felt very special."

Thorne's visit gave Kaki a new lease on life. Because her need to interact with an animal had been so great, and because she overcame her fear to experience that interaction, she had discovered that she could survive leaving her apartment. She began to attend bingo games, went shopping with friends and, in general, took back her life. She told everyone it was because of Thorne, that he had given her the courage she needed.

Barb feels certain that other healings took place in the retirement home as well. "I took the dog there a couple of times. If I happened to have him in the car and didn't bring him in, the residents would make me go back and get him. If he wasn't with me, people always asked about him."

The day we were scheduled to meet with Barb and get this

story down on tape, Steve e-mailed me with the news that Thorne had taken seriously ill. By that afternoon, he was dead, the victim of a rare blood disorder at two and a half years old. We can only offer thanks for the gift of Thorne and trust that some other mission took this angel to a level we cannot, as yet, see, and only barely understand.

"We know that fear is inappropriate whenever it limits a person's capacity for a normal life," Michael said. "In other words, when it becomes an obstacle to having a relationship, keeping a job, or being able to relax and socialize. There's no one set of patterns; it's different for everyone. In Kaki's case, her life was completely encumbered by her fear. Such terror would look pretty unreasonable to others, but for Kaki it had become her way of life—until Thorne, a true animal angel."

There is a reason why dogs are considered man's best friend. Dogs have been at man's side longer than any other animal. The connection between the two has rendered them virtually inseparable. What child growing up does not have or want a puppy? Man has so altered the original wolf or coyote, from which the dog descended, that today's creatures are almost more man's creation than nature's.

Companionship and loyalty are the values of dog totems and they certainly fit. We have all heard stories of the incredible abuse some dogs take. Almost always, they crawl back to their masters on their bellies, offering the owners one more chance to change and love, offering their bodies as sacrifices to these needy, hurtful people so that other people do not suffer in their stead. How many angels have suffered earthly pain and lack of love in order to provide a psychic release for someone who doesn't know better? What might the world be like were it not for these remarkable angels? I shudder to think.

Jez and the Beagle

Jez, a beautiful, young, blond mother was entering a scary time in her life. Her marriage of ten years was falling apart. Her husband, whom she believed to be a workaholic, had become such a stranger that he had never even met many of her friends. She had been unhappy for many years, but it was the only life she knew. She grew anxious and upset, and worried about how she would make a living. She worried about ruining her little girls' lives. She herself was the daughter of a divorced marriage and wasn't at all sure she wanted to do that to her children.

Jez was coming apart. She could not act, and was scared to death of what would become of her. She began therapy with one of Michael's colleagues and joined the next Natural Awakenings workshop that Michael held in Florida.

"Michael assigned us the task of going for a nature walk," Jez remembered. "We were supposed to go out and connect with the earth and get whatever messages came our way, to be aware of animals and plants, any natural phenomenon."

Jez was not opposed to nature at all. But her relationship to animals hadn't always been happy because of her experiences as a teenager. When she was thirteen, her father's wife resembled Cinderella's cruel stepmother. She never accepted her husband's children, and the relationship between them was never good.

"My stepmother's brother still lived in their family house," Jez explained. "And he took care of the family dog, a big white dog, part chow and part shepherd. He was ferocious. When you came to the house, he'd be waiting by the gate, foaming at the mouth, ready to attack you. I grew up knowing how vicious that dog was."

One day when Jez was visiting her step-uncle, her stepmother decided to prove to Jez the dog was completely under her control. "She insisted I come into the room where this dog was. I was cowering in the other room, my heart racing and not wanting anything to do with that ferocious beast." Her stepmother insisted, however, and Jez walked into the room, quaking with fear.

"She didn't have him on a leash or anything and the dog seemed happy and cheerful when I walked in. He was playing with my dad and stepmother. But when he turned to look at me, his whole attitude changed. I saw it in his eyes."

Before anyone could move, the dog snarled and leaped at Jez, pinning her to the wall. She felt his teeth closing on her throat just as her father managed to pull him off. "I flipped out completely," Jez said.

Unbelievably, her stepmother wanted to prove the same thing

again the next week, insisting that she would keep the dog on a leash this time and that the animal was in her perfect control.

"I was standing in the kitchen shaking with fear," Jez remembers. "But it's one of the few times my dad stood up to her. He told her no, he wouldn't make me come into the room with the dog. She was so mad she ran into the garage and started pulling shelves down with glass and breaking stuff all over the place. It was very dramatic. That was the final straw for Dad. He ended up leaving her." Many years later, her father found, and married, his perfect soul mate. Watching him with the love of his life finally made Jez realize what her own marriage was missing and gave her the courage to want more from a relationship.

The whole episode with the brutish dog had much more of an impact on Jez's life than she could have dreamed. At the time, it was the most frightening experience of her life. "I'm still scared of dogs today," she said. "It takes me a long time to warm up to dogs."

On her walk during a Natural Awakenings workshop, Jez found a field overlooking a lake and lay down on her back in the tall, dry grass. "The smell of hay was intoxicating," she said. "I lay watching the light dance on the lake and a great blue heron stalking prey. It was so deadly silent." Her choice of words was informative, and not coincidentally, it showed where her mind was. Her life was deadly silent. Afraid to move forward, afraid to go back, she was frozen by her own fears.

"I lay there, trying to go deep inside and find who I was," she said. "I'd lost all my perspective and definition. Who am I separate from wife and mother? Separate from everyone's expectations of who I should be? As I lay there, feeling the support and warmth of the earth, I found my fears. My heart was breaking; I was desperately afraid of the future. I wanted to believe I could step forward and make a change, but was so afraid I couldn't move. I felt absolutely frozen."

Jez cried into the grass. She wanted to scream but was even afraid of disturbing the tranquility of the scene.

The earth herself is a healer. At last, Jez calmed down, aware of some semblance of peace, if not resolve. It was time to return to the group. Exhausted, she rose on wobbly legs and looked around at the scene. The heron was still stalking prey. Slowly, she turned and walked to the end of the lake and into the woods.

Suddenly, from far off, a dog suddenly began to bark fiercely. Her heart pounded and she hurried to get through the woods and back onto the road. The barking grew louder. From the corner of her eye, she caught sight of a large, white German shepherd racing straight for her, lips curled in a snarl. "It was like my childhood all over again," Jez said.

Completely panic-stricken, Jez ran for her life, her heart racing, palms sweating, legs pounding the earth faster than they ever had before. Frantically, she looked for the road, the path out of the wilderness. In her fear she felt the ground trembling beneath the onslaught of the dog's charge, heard the gnashing of teeth, and could almost feel the heat of the animal's breath on her flesh.

At some point, the sound faded away, but Jez raced on, unable to stop. She finally saw the dirt road and emerged from the woods gasping for breath, shaking and sobbing. She chanced a quick glance behind, saw nothing, and turned to hurry back along the road. Suddenly, she gasped, her heart leaped at the sight of another dog. She stopped short, her breath catching in her throat.

A happy, tail-wagging beagle gazed up at her. Jez took a shaky breath, then continued on down the road. The beagle trotted along at her side. "Oddly enough, I wasn't afraid of this dog at all," she said. "He seemed to be there as a protector, a guide. He stayed with me all the way to the end of the road. When I reached the turn-off to go back to the group, he simply disappeared. I looked back and couldn't see him anywhere."

Jez was still shaking, but when she returned to the group, she knew that she was safe. She also found instant recognition. When she shared the experience with the other group members, she realized that the shepherd represented her fears of the unknown. "You know, when I think about it today, I'm not even sure I saw a white shepherd; all I know was that it was a big dog." And that big *white* dog represented the most fearful thing she'd ever faced: her stepmother's ferocious dog.

She knew that the beagle was an angel. It changed her life forever. "I knew then that though my path may be filled with frightening things, I will always be protected and watched over," she said.

Jez went through what was ultimately a nasty divorce with strength and conviction. She fought the battles she needed to fight for her children and moved north. There she is developing a completely new relationship with nature, one that she enjoys sharing by writing to her friends in the South who have watched her grow and change in strength and beauty.

"This experience completely turned Jez's life around," Michael said. "She was under a very real threat of losing everything, including herself. She was doing a lot of personal work. And that German shepherd *is* real; it's chased people before. But no one knows where the beagle came from. No one who lives around there has ever seen that beagle." Michael shrugs. "I'm sure it was real. And it was definitely on a mission to help Jez. It was a true animal angel."

As a side note, the heron was an important symbol as well. The heron, by its very nature, represents patience, but it also represents self-determination and self-reliance, the very qualities Jez most needed just then. "The heron can also see through distortion," Michael pointed out. "The heron fishes across the surface of the water, where water meets air and everything is distorted at that intersection. When you watch a heron hunting, you'll see it shift its head side to side, analyzing the distortion and the reality of what it's seeing. The heron knows to stab not where the fish *appears* to be, but where it really is. Herons are masters at seeing what really is. And there was Jez, lying in the grass, trying to work through all the distortions of her life.

"It's exciting to recognize a sign from nature," he continued. "And it's good to scrutinize it, to stop and reflect, 'What was I thinking about when that happened? What emotional state was I in?' You can come up with a reasonable self-assessment connected to that event. But the other part is the volunteering. That's when we're not looking for a sign, but it comes anyway. Everybody's initial story is his or her most angelic. After it happens a time or two, you start looking for them."

The exact breed of dog that impacts a person certainly means something in itself. Kaki needed a big, powerful dog. Perhaps that was necessary to overcome a big, powerful fear. A yappy little ball of fluff would not have worked for her. On the other hand, another big, powerful dog might have sent Jez into another spasm of terror. Yet, lest anyone overlook the other worthy animal in Jez's story, the German shepherd was also an angel. It took the shepherd for the beagle to have any value. It took the shepherd to scare Jez so badly that she was able to go back and face childhood fears, and thereby, move past her present-day fears. Wherever it is that angels get their assignments, the beagle got the easy job; the shepherd got the tough one. Some animal has to fill the tough job, and it probably isn't as much fun from the angelic point of view. But both are equally necessary. It is the same for people.

Michael laughed as he recounted his own heron validation story. "I think I've seen a heron every day of my life. To me the message of the heron is patience. But when I first started working with the concept, and confronted the idea that these herons were animal angels, I still was skeptical and kind of explained away the constant presence of the heron by attributing it to the fact that I lived around water. About six years ago a group of us made a trip to Sedona, Arizona. At one point everyone decided to go shopping, which isn't my thing. I was just going along with the gang, but inside I was sort of grumbling. So there I was, in downtown Sedona, in the middle of the desert and a huge shadow passed over us. I assumed it would be an eagle, so I looked up and there was this blue heron flying overhead, going flap, flap, flap. I just had to laugh. I was being told to have patience. At that time I also needed patience for some personal issues in my life with which I was dealing in the workshop."

Michael didn't question his animal angels concept again. But he still had to acquire his own learning curve of recognition.

Michael remembers the very first Natural Awakenings workshop he did in a newly revised format. Originally, he held several in the forest, simply using nature as a backdrop. Analyzing the results of those workshops, he fine-tuned and tinkered and came up with a format he still uses today. Although the overall format remains the same, each workshop is unique; each has its own flavor. The people and the animals that show up are all part of the workshop. Michael freely admits he has little control over this aspect. This is God's part. In the early days of this workshop dynamic, Michael still found lessons to learn.

At first, each workshop was given a name in a follow-up newsletter sent to the participants. The first one was called the Coral Snake Workshop.

"I was preparing for the workshop one weekend, busy doing all the things I have to do to get ready. I'm working in the yard, cleaning up and I rake some leaves over and there's a coral snake, about twenty-four inches long. Naturally I didn't want to kill it, but I didn't want to take a chance of someone getting bitten either. So I decided to bag it, and take it someplace else later."

At this point in time, Michael had just begun paying attention to animal signs in new way. He put the snake in an old pillowcase and hung it from a hook under a shaded porch eave where they usually hung potted plants. "People started arriving and unpacking their things, settling in for the weekend. When we first gathered in the circle and were doing introductions, I let everybody know not to mess with the bag under the porch, that there was a coral snake inside.

"Well, everybody was instantly horrified, or fascinated and wondered why I hadn't killed it. I explained I didn't want them to step on it or sit on it and get hurt, that I was guarding them from potential harm, but I didn't wish harm to the snake either. Then I showed everybody the snake so they would know what a poisonous snake looked like and we began the workshop."

Saturday morning, Michael, as usual, was the first one up to fix breakfast for the crew. As he rattled around in the kitchen, some of the lessons he passed on to others were running through his head, specifically, lessons about being mindful and aware. "As I wandered around, I suddenly got this brainstorm that the coral snake was supposed to be part of the weekend. I wasn't supposed to interfere with what God had sent to teach us and interact with us. I took the bag off the hook, untied it and put the snake back where I'd found it.

"After breakfast we began the opening ceremony and I said, 'Oh, by the way, the coral snake is back in the yard,' and I flipped the bag out into the circle. Their eyes got really big. We heard things like, 'Oh my God, I'm not going outside.' Then I explained what a wonderful message the coral snake was. You have to really be NOT looking to step on a coral snake. The snake is red, yellow and black. How much more obvious can any message from nature be? The group had already seen the snake and knew exactly what it looked like so I advised them to just keep their eyes open, to be aware, and be mindful of where they went and what they did."

As in every Natural Awakenings workshop, the group did some exercises, then took a break. People wandered onto the concrete patio outside the back door. A couple of ladies stepped into the grass, then suddenly remembered and jumped back. "I advised them to trust their own judgment," Michael said. "Now that they knew the snake was there, they wouldn't have any trouble watching where they stepped." Gradually they all got braver and did venture into the yard and on into the woods as the weekend progressed."

At the end of every workshop, processing the whole experience is the last exercise. "Several people talked about the coral snake and how it had caused them to be far more alert. They really felt that the message from the snake was not to be afraid, but to be observant and avoid danger when it is known. Even though they started out afraid, by the end of the weekend they had less fear of the snake and the whole outdoors than they had before they ever knew about the snake. They had begun to trust that they *could* see things and *could* take care of themselves." The group members also spoke of a heightened awareness that allowed them to see more than they'd ever seen before in the outdoors. It was very exciting for them. They didn't think they'd ever view nature, or their own roles in it, in the same way again.

Another important aspect of fear is the power of fear. From an energetic point of view, our minds are so powerful that when we focus on our fears, we can actually make them happen. We call to us our greatest fears. Why do our minds work this way? The answer: so that we can overcome them. Only by facing our fears do we overcome them.

What animal might you think of when you think of fear? Things that dart and hide from possible predators? Mice. Rabbits. As already mentioned, fear can be a good thing. Learning how to protect oneself when in true danger is a valuable skill, and this is something that rabbits can teach. Freezing so as to become invisible, hiding in tall grass and thickets, planning escape routes and rapid, sporadic movements are all wonderfully positive lessons the rabbit can teach. But sometimes, a rabbit may show up simply to point out that you are afraid.

Alice and the Rabbit

When Alice's teenage son was arrested on drug charges, she was devastated. Alice had watched her son change during the last year and felt him slipping away from her. He was rebellious and angry. She could no longer relate to him, despite years of closeness. She had raised her only child as a single mom and this change was hurting them both. But Alice had never dreamed her son would end up in court. And she certainly never dreamed that she might be part of the cause.

Alice, a teacher, had always been involved in metaphysics. She had done a lot of reflecting upon her situation with her son, feeling plenty of guilt and worry about her role in his life. "When he was arrested, I wrote him a letter saying that I felt that all my worry and fear this past year had helped create this situation. I know very well about fears actualizing themselves. So I apologized to him for whatever part I may have played in getting him to this point, and, of course, I professed my love and support."

The next morning as Alice pulled out of her garage to go to work, a dead rabbit lay in the middle of her driveway. "I was horrified. I knew it was affirming the fact that I had called my own fears back to me," she said. "I went back and checked the medicine cards for more meaning. Then I decided to do some crafting work that would focus on a positive outcome for my son's release."

In Native American cultures "crafting work" means creating a medicine piece. A medicine piece is any personally created craft, artwork, prayer tie, etc., which, is symbolic of the prayer you are praying during its creation. In other words, it is a visible manifestation of your prayer. It doesn't have to be pretty or perfect. Afterward, it may be gifted, worn, buried, burned or sent off to sea, whatever you feel is appropriate for that piece.

The next day, there were still a few remains of the rabbit in Alice's driveway. Alice took this to mean that she still had a few little bits of fear left. So she worked on her medicine piece again. That was the day her son was due in court. "When I arrived and first saw him in shackles and that orange jumpsuit," Alice said, shaking her head, "oh my God, what it feels like to see your son that way. It was so painful. But they did not send him back to the juvenile detention center. Instead, they released him to me."

For Alice, it was a clear message about the power of fears and the importance of redirecting them. Later, she realized it was far more than that.

"Alice was calling her fears to her," Michael explained. "But the real, core fear is not about her son ending up in jail or worse. It's the eternal problem of mothers and sons. It is the father's job in any animal society to kick the son out of the herd or group or house. It is the mother's job to nurture and cling and let the child know she is always there. Both parental jobs are very important, vitally necessary. In Alice's case, there was no father to do the job and it was not in her nature to push her son away, especially when he had been her primary family relationship for many years. Every step Alice took to try to rectify her fear was another attempt to keep him from escaping her sphere, her influence. She wouldn't be able to mother him and protect him anymore.

"Her letter was one more attempt, a secret way to bring him back to her, to continue to hold power over him. Meanwhile, on some innate but unconscious level, her son is recognizing that it was the time in life when he needed to separate from her. Her perfect mothering, her sweetness, her love is like a giant magnet, like a gravitational pull. He's fueling up a rocket and the more Mom held on, the better she took care of him, the more fuel he had to put into this rocket to escape her gravity."

It could be added that it is often a son's job to fight his father for a while before he goes off and leaves the safety of home. And that in this case, with no father to push against, the police often act as pseudo fathers. This is not an uncommon dynamic in fatherless families.

Alice became a client of Michael's and she has been working diligently to understand this issue. "I am struggling through the delicate dance of letting my son experience and be responsible for the natural and logical consequences of his own decisions and actions," Alice said. She finally recognizes that her fear is the fear of all mothers, that of losing her son, by death or by his going off into a dangerous world without her umbrella of protection.

The subject of parenting comes up throughout many of the issues of life. "It is mom's job to teach love, trust, acceptance," Michael said. "Dad's job is to teach respect, honor, competition and to provide a safe practice field for the child to learn on, making sure the playing field is level, the fight is fair.

"If you take karate, horseback riding, or gymnastic lessons, one of the first things you learn is how to hit the mat and not get hurt or how to roll with the punches. You know that falls, mishaps and other dangers are going to happen, and the idea of trying to prevent them is ludicrous. Teaching your child how to deal with danger is important. Teaching them to avoid danger only passes on the denials of the parents.

"Somewhere between sixteen and nineteen is about a year-long window of opportunity for youngsters to 'leave the home' in a healthy way, psychologically and emotionally, if not physically. If they leave home during that time, it's usually a smooth process. But if the parent worries and holds on and it goes beyond that time period, or if you try to do it for them, they become crippled, and they can't fly. It's just like breaking open the cocoon for a butterfly. If the cocoon doesn't open naturally, the butterfly's wings won't ever unfold and instead of helping it along, you've crippled it."

Sparrows are one of the most commonplace of animals. Tiny, nondescript birds, they are everywhere, literally everywhere in the world. Yet their commonness and their diminutive size are the very reasons that they traditionally have been the symbol of ordinary people surviving, or even overcoming, powerful forces. In Europe, folk tales abound of the tiny sparrow surviving the eagle, the hawk and the fox. These stories gave the peasants hope that they too might survive the powerful, the big and the ruthless. Fear may be the most powerful of our enemies, but stories of transient sparrows help to assuage frightening thoughts.

The following story will be appreciated by anybody who has

ever gone offshore on a boat. The stories of land birds blown offshore and seeking refuge on boats are as old as sailing ships themselves. It was this story that first showed Michael the power of animal teachings.

Marjorie and the Sparrow

Marjorie is a psychotherapist from the northeast. Now in her early fifties, for many years she has pursued an interest in spiritual teachings through the study of both eastern religions and Native American traditions.

"When I first told this story," Marjorie said. "I told it as a teaching tool. I've used it a lot since then, because people are often moved to tears by it."

In September of 1996, Marjorie and her husband, Bjorn, took a tour they had taken many times before. "We went to an island in Canada called Grand Manan Island in the Bay of Fundy in New Brunswick, where Canada meets Maine. Campobello Island, where Franklin Delano Roosevelt had a 'cottage,' is nearby. It's a popular area for birdwatchers and whale watchers because the tides are twenty-six feet high, and there's a lot of activity and a lot of food. Whenever we go there we always go whale watching on a lobster boat with local people. Because of the fishing quota, they can't make a living fishing anymore, so they've been trying to offer tourism activities. Fortunately, because it's so remote, it hasn't really been gentrified yet.

"We go a long way offshore on the whale watching trip. At least, it's wilderness to me, out of sight of land. It feels like the wildlife invites us into their home. It's a lovely experience."

The trip is a true paradise of nature observation. The Bay of Fundy is one of the few places where northern right whales mate. "There are only about 350 of them left," Marjorie said. "They're very curious and will come right up to the boat. We've actually been behind them when they were mating. That was terrific.

"The finwhales are very shy, about eighty feet long. You always see them blowing in the distance. They don't get too near the boat. And then of course there are the humpback whales. They get very close; we've had them go under the boat."

Each time Marjorie and her husband took the whale watching trip, birdwatchers made up a number of the passengers. "One time, in fact, when we were way out, we saw two hummingbirds fly by. We thought, 'How can this be?' I found out very recently that they ride on the wind currents."

That particular September day was foggy. "The fog is good," the captain said. "It will keep us warm." Puffins floated on the surface of the water all around the boat. They were three hours out, in the middle of the ocean, when a tiny sparrow fluttered, utterly exhausted, to the transom of the boat.

"The captain told us they call such birds 'hitchhikers,'" Marjorie explained. "They get blown offshore, and they get so tired trying to fight their way back to land, they need someplace to touch down for a while. The birdwatchers warned us not to scare the sparrow because it needed to rest."

Suddenly, in the midst of the breathtaking sight of breaching and blowing whales, all of the passengers, twenty people, were riveted by the plight of one tiny brown bird. "I was struck by how quickly everyone's attention had been captured," Marjorie said. "All of this magnificent splendor everywhere, yet every person was focused on the plight of this miniscule bird. It looked so vulnerable. I kept watching it and wondering why on earth it was so far out to sea.

"The captain tried to maneuver the boat to keep the sparrow out of the wind. The bird watchers and wildlife rehabilitation people tried to feed it. The captain and everyone were so gentle. That really touched me too."

Yet the tiny bird, panting and trembling with exhaustion, was so anxious it fluttered from one resting place to another, becoming more exhausted. Suddenly, it flew to Bjorn's hand. "When it landed, it looked straight up at me," Marjorie said. "My husband has nice energy and I thought, *It will feel safe now*, and I made soft, soothing sounds to it. I felt like I connected to the sparrow."

It was when Marjorie said to the bird, "I love you," that it flew out over the water and dropped into the sea.

"I was stunned," Marjorie said. "Why should it have flown off just then, when it was so safe? We tried everything to rescue it. I'd never before seen what happens to a bird that isn't a water bird when it lands in the water. The captain backed up the boat and the mate tried to scoop the bird up in a bucket but it was scared and kept fluttering away."

Helplessly, everyone watched as the bird's wings got heavier and heavier every time it tried to lift itself out of the water. Finally, completely exhausted, the little bird's head dropped into the water. Complete silence reigned as every passenger watched the sparrow sink beneath the water's surface, most of them crying.

Two different parts of Marjorie's personality responded to the situation. Her clinical self was struck by the dynamics of how this one little bird so impacted everyone on the vessel. But her heart and body grieved. "I knew there was a lesson there," she said. "And I also knew that it was aimed at me. I know that I've had a hard time accepting love and support in my life. I'm so afraid of closeness, I've often pushed people away."

"I know that this was given to me as a teaching, to help others realize that fear is the real enemy. Your fears can kill you. That bird was so safe, so cared for. But it didn't believe it and died because of its fear. I'm really trying to overcome my fears now."

"At the time she saw the sparrow, Marjorie was already working on the aspects of how fear was limiting her. She was participating with friends, working with her husband and letting people near her," Michael said. "She definitely took the message. She knew the sparrow was telling her that she was going to die, at least spiritually, if she did not do something about this fear of letting people participate in her life. The realization hit her hard. Now that she uses it as a teaching instrument, she has found that her experience impacts listeners strongly."

Indeed, the impact was so great that when Michael Rebel first heard this story in a workshop Marjorie was helping to conduct, and saw the impression it made on other "hardened" therapists in the room, he instantly recognized the value of such animal angel teachings. He knew that he wanted to find similar stories that would help more people.

Michael remembered an experience earlier in his life that strengthened his resolve, and offered a lesson in what can happen when one is not limited by fear. It occurred at a time when Michael was struggling to redefine his work as a therapist. He went out on his own as a commercial fisherman seeking truth, healing and solace in the one thing that had always brought him joy, fishing.

Michael and the Sparrow

"I was seventy miles offshore in the Gulf of Mexico on my boat, *Spirit*," he recounts. "A sixteen year old named Paul was working as my deckhand on that particular trip. He was really connected with nature. We were way out, far from the sight of land for a day or two when we heard this 'chirp chirp chirp' and started looking around the boat. We finally found a little field sparrow up on the prow of the boat. We just left it alone and went back to fishing. It kept chirping and hopping around and gradually worked its way onto the back deck. We left the cabin door open with the idea that if it came back, we'd try to gently persuade it to go into the cabin and close the door. From the beginning, the bird wasn't very afraid, and came right around us. So sure enough, it eventually made it into the cabin and we shut the door."

Michael told Paul not to get his hopes up. His experience working on fishing boats in years past had been that by the time a land bird gets up the courage to land on a boat, it's already exhausted beyond the point of recovery. "I've seen thirty, forty birds dead on the deck of a boat every night, blown out by some storm or another. The few who are alive usually refuse food and water, because they're so scared, and die later."

The little sparrow disappeared somewhere inside the cabin for a few hours. They discovered it hiding under paperwork on a table. Unwilling to give up, Paul put bread and water on the table and they continued their fishing.

"The next morning was just amazing," Michael said. "The bird was in there eating the bread and water. Paul and I were both excited. We still had another day and a half of fishing, so we kept the door shut so the bird wouldn't fly out and exhaust itself again. After a couple of hours, the bird had completely explored and accommodated itself to the cabin. It was fine, no problem whatsoever. The sparrow's favorite place was some electronic wiring up on the dash. It got used to us coming and going. It got to where the bird didn't even fly as we came through the door. It adapted very rapidly."

The next day Michael was doing something on the back deck when he looked into the cabin. "Paul had made himself a cheese sandwich, was sitting at the table eating it and the bird was sitting in front of him on the table. Every time Paul took a bite of the sandwich and put it down again, the bird would dash over and grab a bite!"

Michael began recalling Marjorie's story as well as Charlene's story of a cattle egret that landed on a sailboat she was on in the middle of the Gulf of Mexico. The exhausted egret actually walked down the steps from the center cockpit and into the main salon below decks where it remained for the duration of the passage. When the boat made its destination of Isla de Mujeres, Mexico, the bird walked back up on deck and flew off.

"I saw immediately that this sparrow was the antithesis of Marjorie's sparrow," Michael said. "This sparrow story was about what life can be like when you do not let your fears run your life."

The *Spirit* steamed back to shore, the bird busy being a boat bird and seemingly content. "We started coming up the channel, passed spoil islands and were tootling along at a good clip and the bird wasn't paying any attention," Michael said. "Then we started to go past real land, the mainland, and the bird saw it. It started chirping and flitting around the cabin and making the most joyful sounds. We could see that the bird was excited and energized. We wanted to show people the sparrow so we gave it a ride all the way to the boathouse. As we unloaded the fish on the dock, everybody came by to see the little bird. Then we opened the cabin door and the sparrow flew off."

"This incident illustrates what life can be like without fear. When you have flexible rules and expectations, when you can adapt to changing situations, life can be a like an open, adventurous road! There's always new vistas to see and new things to do, some resource available as these birds found out. He was an angel to us and we were angels to him. It was a tradeoff. It was very clear to me that that's exactly what a healthy person would do too."

Fear can be paralyzing, stifling, and traumatizing at certain times in everyone's life. Animal angels can help us overcome irrational, unwanted fear, but we need to remain observant and emotionally open to their influence and the lessons they impart.

chapter three

Guilt

Ordaining every cause for life or death,
Guarding this tattered robe we call the Sky,
Say, am I sinful? Are you not my Master?
Who sins when You alone created me?
　　　—The Rubbaiyyat of Omar Khayaam

"Guilt is a serious disease in our society," Michael said. "You can't be responsible for anything that is out of your control. Guilt is a learned feeling. It's not real. The imaginary positive is that you're responsible. The imaginary negative is that you feel guilty. But they're both illusions."

According to many philosophers, there is only one true guilt and that is recognition of the life lost. This is believing or doing something which, if one had only known better, one would have done differently. Every other guilt feeling is a conditioned response.

If we do something wrong, the response should be that we correct it, apologize for it, or acknowledge it in some way and then go on with our lives. But many of us can't do that. We carry a burden that is either put there by someone else or self-imposed. Feeling responsible is a way of feeling in control, even of feeling important. It usually is not a conscious thought, however, and therein lies the pain.

"Guilt has been prevalent in our society for so long that it may be reaching the point of being passed on genetically," Michael added. "It's really hard to get people to realize that they cannot control each and every thing that happens. In a way, it's a delusion of grandeur to feel that way, even though the grandeur feels like low self-esteem to the person who is experiencing it."

Guilt may often cover up fear. This is fear of reprisal for bad deeds, or more often, fear of judgment. Ultimately, though rarely in conscious thought, this can be distilled to the fear of the judgment of God, particularly if we believe we have harmed something in his creation. But then, what is not of his creation?

One of his creations, the spider, is another very old symbol, appearing in cultural legends the world over. Considered the storyteller and dream weaver in many Native American cultures, the spider represents the weaving of anything, from illusion and fate to the very wheel of life itself.

Melinda and the Spider

Melinda is a nature-loving businesswoman who lives with her husband, J.J., on the edge of the wilderness so that she can enjoy the nature she loves and still be able to conduct her business. New to southern flora, fauna and ecology, since moving south only two years ago, she has been fascinated with every new thing she has discovered. She has also been intrigued by some of the new things she has learned about herself and about the universe in general since seeking therapeutic help with Michael.

"Emotionally and physically, I was in pretty bad shape while I still lived up north," she explained. "I'd been so caught up in the corporate world that not only did I have no time for nature or leisure, but I was making myself sick."

Melinda was a self-described workaholic. She had to be. For many years she was a single mother, desperate to provide home and security for her children. Like too many single parents, nothing else existed for her. Melinda paid the price with her health. Her sister was a friend of Michael's and for the first six months of Melinda's serious health problems, her sister begged her to come south where she lived to meet some of the alternative health providers she knew. After finding that traditional medicine only made things worse, Melinda finally gave in and bought a ticket to Florida. Her sister didn't even recognize the haggard and gray woman who hobbled off the plane with canes and braces. "She took me around to several healers of various types," Melinda said, "and then she introduced me to Michael."

When both her sister and Michael suggested that Melinda's lifestyle had contributed to her plague of health problems, she was astonished to instantly recognize the truth of it. That realization connected her to both of them in such a way that she could never turn back to her old way of thinking. Already experiencing improvement in her health, she went home after one week, without canes or braces, ready to explore things anew.

Like others, however, she found that she could not maintain her new belief system while surrounded by old places and things, old friends and old ideas. Melinda loved her relatives and friends, but they didn't understand the new things she was learning.

She had quit working altogether, but her health did not improve. Finally, her health deteriorated to the point that she was compelled to make the ultimate shift, a permanent move away from family, home, job and friends. Rarely had anything been as painful as this process, but her body and mind improved almost as soon as she returned to Florida. She realized that along with the spiritual healing she'd experienced there, the warm climate had also healed her. Eventually, Melinda met J.J. and married him. Since her arrival in Florida, she continues to believe that she made the only choice—to move south—she could at that time.

One afternoon, after living in Florida for several years, while walking to her washing machine in the shed outside the house where she was living, Melinda noticed a magnificent spider web on the outside of the porch. It was anchored to the outside walls by about six strands and was anchored on the neighbor's house by only a few strands as well. The web's support was from a tree branch that was about twenty-five feet from the roof of the shed.

"It was one of those classic webs that was perfectly designed, about two by three feet, hanging at an angle that made the morning dew gathered on its strands sparkle. It was dazzling," she said. "I pointed it out to my neighbor and he admired it too."

She noted that the spider, which she had not yet seen, might have its job cut out for it. The wind had been kicking up leaves and moss which deposited nicely into the web, transforming it into a net, but the debris detracted from the ability of the web to perform its main function—that of capturing dinner for its maker.

Like the spider, often called the housekeeper of the world, Melinda hurried out several days later to do laundry again, forgetting about the web. She bumped into it, breaking three strands of the anchor holding it to the shed. "I was surprised at how strong those strands were," she said. She was also surprised at the feelings of sorrow that arose, and it stung her to be the destroyer of such a masterpiece. Yet, about an hour later, with her mind on other things, she returned to pick up the laundry, again forgetting the web. This time, she ripped apart the entire thing. Now she was really upset. That beautiful web was gone. "I hadn't yet seen the spider, but I felt like a brute destroying it, even unwittingly," she said.

As she worked through the rest of the day, she realized that her destruction of the spider's home was arousing stronger feelings in her than seemed to be warranted. In typical fashion, though, she tried to stay busy and not focus on the sadness.

At dusk, Melinda, grateful that she now worked only part-time and had time to relax and contemplate, sat in the chair on the porch to watch the remaining daylight leave the sky. She saw the remaining strand of web floating from the treetop. A few leaves were attached to it and at first she didn't see anything but the dancing of the leaves within the strand. Then she saw the spider riding the biggest leaf on the remaining strand of silver string.

"Its body was about the size of a quarter," Melinda said. "No wonder that web was so strong, coming from such a hefty critter!" As the wind blew that lone strand and the spider continued to ride it, it looked like the spider was using the leaf to try to find another anchor for its web.

As Melinda watched, hoping the spider could reattach the web to the laundry shed, she suddenly had a memory. "It blew me away," she said. "I hadn't thought of it for years, but when I was a little girl, I was terrified of spiders!" Because she has no such fear today, this sudden memory sent shock waves throughout her system as she sat there, recalling the exact incident.

She wasn't always afraid. "When I was about seven years old, a girlfriend and I were fascinated by the different spider web designs and egg cases and food sacs that spiders created. We spent one whole summer collecting spiders and egg cases. My family had an old shed, something like the shed here, that no one else used so we used it. We began collecting spiders!"

In mason jars, glass aquariums and any other container they could find, Melinda and her friend placed every spider "thing" they found. "We had a truly remarkable collection of spiders and spider egg sacs," Melinda remembered. "We learned a lot about the spiders we collected and we thought them so beautiful. For a whole summer we just concentrated on spiders."

When winter came, Melinda and her girlfriend forgot all about their project. It would be spring before they remembered their wonderful collection from the summer before. When they thought of it, they ran to the shed, opened the door and peered inside.

"All of the glass of the Mason jars and aquariums had broken during the winter," Melinda said. "We stepped into a dank cave of spider webs. Spider babies fell from the ceiling, from the walls, from every corner. Many layers of dead spiders were on the floor." All Melinda could see were the dead spiders, seemingly the result of her neglect. It was a haunting, horrid nightmare for a little girl who once thought spiders so intriguing.

The girls' parents cleaned out the shed, but Melinda never went back into it again. For many, many years she could not look at a spider without replaying that scene in her head over and over again. "I woke with tears and nightmares many, many times," she said, her voice choked up even today.

In retrospect, Melinda recognizes that she also saw many live babies. "Maybe if my parents had encouraged me to help with the cleaning, I could have seen that so many of the babies *were* still alive..."

She shrugged. "But I'm sure they were only thinking of protecting me then. All I knew at the time was that I was responsible for so many spider deaths." And somehow, over the following years, that huge guilt turned into a fear of spiders.

As Melinda remembered this memory over the next few days, she watched gratefully as the spider rebuilt her web, this time a little higher so that passers-by could not destroy it so easily. "The spread of the web itself was probably about four feet," Melinda said. "The strands that held it to the live oak and the shed must be ten or fifteen feet long."

Melinda continued to process all these feelings of guilt as she watched the spider rebuild its web. At last it came to her. "I suddenly realized I was relating it to the same kind of destruction I felt responsible for when I suddenly packed up and left my kids to move south.

"At the time, I was as desperate and scared as I'd ever been in my life," she admitted. "I didn't know if I'd ever work again. I'd always been vital, full of energy and I'd work eighty hour weeks, healthy as a horse most of my life. When my system finally broke down, it broke down all the way, and I had no tools to help me know how to deal with that. I'd never been in that position before and it scared me. Nothing had ever scared me like that illness did."

But to her family—and to her—the timing could not have been worse. Her four children suddenly had to be on their own. Although they were young adults, they were all just beginning to move outside the home. She still was their anchor. She and her oldest daughter-in-law had just purchased property together where Melinda would have had a house of her own and helped make their dreams come true.

"When I made the decision to move to Florida, none of my children could understand it. I had cashed in my life chips on work and then, when I actually had an opportunity to spend time with my family, even if it was because of my poor health, I was leaving them. From my children's viewpoint, I destroyed their home base, their web!"

It would still be a few days before Melinda would get a close enough look at the spider to identify the species. Meanwhile, she and her husband watched the spider's dark silhouette every evening as it descended to carefully weed out any leaves or debris that gathered in the web during the day.

"Unless the dew or the light was on the web, you couldn't see it," Melinda said. "I pointed it out to another neighbor one day when the sunlight hit it at just the right angle so that you could see the strong strands, but not the web. He was amazed. I have had those strong strands in my face and was amazed as well! Sometimes after a rain storm, we'd see the sparkling of the entire web coated with drops of water. What a beautiful sight!"

One day, one of the daily summer thunderstorms threw a huge handful of Spanish moss into the web. "It looked odd hanging there seemingly in mid air. The weight of it took down two sides and the web hung at a broken angle instead of the lovely hammock it had been for the past week. I wanted to go pull the moss out of the web to help the spider, but luckily I had a moment of brilliant insight and realized I would probably pull down the whole web, while she could untangle the moss one string at a time. So I left the job to her."

And the spider did exactly that. Working one strand at a time, the moss was gradually cleared away. "She, and I began to think of her as a female, cleaned house so efficiently that I was put to shame since mine was so bad," Melinda said, laughing. "Every evening I watched her keeping house and doing what comes naturally to a spider. It gave me a fine sense of stability, responsibility, upkeep, all those things that I often complain about because they seem so boring."

As the days went by, Melinda, like the spider, continued to pull out her guilty feelings, one strand at a time. It centered on her move away from her children, and she remembered the intense anger of her youngest child, just heading off for her first year of college and desperately needing to know that home still existed. She recalled the fury of her oldest, with whom she'd spent many hours planning their future home together. And she felt their lack of understanding about why she needed to move. At the time, Melinda was looking through the door of a brand new world and she did not understand herself. Hard put to explain it, all she could do was follow her antennae and go.

Melinda is not afraid of spiders today. But her fear did follow her into young adulthood. Since she loved the outdoors and all of the creatures she encountered, it disturbed her to experience what she considered an irrational fear of such a small animal as a spider. She had forgotten the nightmares and the opening of the door of the shed during her childhood. Only the fear remained. The very sight of a spider sent shudders down her spine. If one were actually to touch her it would elicit tears and an almost overwhelming sense of panic.

When she was twenty, Melinda's first child was born. It was a girl, and like most new parents, Melinda wanted to be the perfect mother to her child, to teach her all the wonderful parts of the world and to protect her from the not-so-wonderful parts. As the baby turned into a toddler, Melinda was confronted with her fears in a way that she had not anticipated. Like her own mother, the toddler thought that ants and worms and all things that moved were the most glorious toys that she had encountered, including spider webs and spiders. "At first, I'd snatch her up whenever she got near a spider. But I always bit my tongue, making sure I didn't scream or cry or call out for help." In wanting to protect her child, Melinda instinctively held back her own fear so as not to pass it on to her daughter.

Gradually, in the old fake-it-till-you-make-it style, Melinda began to sense herself at seven or eight, without fear, as she watched her daughter grow. And gradually her fear of spiders abated.

She began to show her daughter the way the dew sparkled on spider webs outside, and as her daughter began to understand more, Melinda found delight in teaching her what she had long ago learned in her own childhood—the magic of the egg cases and food sacs and the beauty of the creatures themselves. The challenge of raising a youngster to appreciate natural surroundings re-awakened her own youthful fascination, and gradually her fear was broken. She gained understanding that the fear had been the result of a bad experience, not a bad spider. By the time Melinda's second child was born, the healing felt complete. A spider web mobile hung from the baby's crib.

One warm Florida day, Melinda saw enough of the spider that she was able to find its name on the Internet. It was a Giant Lichen Orb-Weaver. She said, "Can you imagine how that name fits this beautiful weaver of circles? An Orb-Weaver: a completer of circles."

Finally, Melinda realized that she had completed her own circle about spiders and guilt. "Look at how I worked through my fear of spiders, because of sheer love for my child and the refusal to pass my fear on to her! I think all the pain and guilt I suffered came from a sense that if I loved my children, I wouldn't have left. It's supposed to be the children that jump out of the nest, but instead, it was me!"

At last, through weeks of watching the spider, Melinda understood some of the pain she had been feeling, and at last she could find peace. "I know I love my children with all my heart. I don't have to prove anything to anybody about that. Leaving them was one of the most painful things I've ever done, but I also recognize now that perhaps it was the right time to do so. We were all so close, and they depended on me so much, that maybe the only way to give them their wings was to remove myself from their presence."

Her new, loving husband, J.J., just happened to be in the right place when the spider was about to meet her end. A wasp was dragging her across the sidewalk into a prepared hole. J.J. called to Melinda and then said comfortingly, "Don't worry honey, she's not dead yet, I'll get her."

Melinda suffered an initial pang, yet said, "No, this is how the world works; it's okay."

They watched as the wasp struggled with its prey. The spider was several times larger than the wasp, so it was quite a struggle. This was the first time they had seen the spider so closely. "She was so beautiful," Melinda said. "Not just the markings on her body, but the striping on her legs that had not been obvious before. But the wasp was quite a display, too. It had iridescent blue/black wings that when opened, revealed a stunning band of orange around its belly. Dragging that spider would be like a human trying to tow a car down the road with his teeth."

Melinda and J.J. had to leave, but returned about an hour and a half later. The wasp was just completing the burial and Melinda sighed at the loss. Yet her love of nature could not help but realize the circle of life she had just witnessed. "Imagine, a wasp has a lifetime of only one season and almost half a day had been spent in capturing and burying the spider," she said. "What could be that important?"

Only one thing in the life of a wasp would be that important: offspring. Her eggs had been laid inside the spider's body and the wasp's young would have food when they hatched. "So the spider will give life to the very enemy that took her from our enjoyment and from her web. But I guarantee you that somewhere up in that monstrous oak tree hangs an egg sack left by our friend," added Melinda with a smile. Both wasp and spider left homes and provision for their young, even as they departed this world.

The death of this one spider left Melinda with a sense of peace that she had not felt since she was seven years old. The fear had been left behind long ago, but there had been a lingering sense of guilt for having captured so many spiders and being a part of their demise. Seeing the entire cycle of this once-feared arachnid allowed Melinda to let go of the final piece of the old shed. The glorious Orb-Weaver helped her to complete a circle of her own, put aside her feelings of guilt and move forward in her life.

"Another way we often use guilt is to mask real feelings," Michael explained. "In Melinda's case, she was probably feeling intense sadness and simply didn't know how to deal with it. Guilt was easier for her to handle at that time. Remember, if you're feeling guilt and it is not about life lost, you are covering up another feeling."

Unlike the relatively small, earth-bound spider, an animal which conveys one of the greatest senses of grandeur is the eagle. No matter the person, place or time, when an eagle soars into view, it is easy to notice that everyone stops what he or she is doing to look. It is difficult to believe that everyone doesn't feel touched by something special, something significant, even, perhaps, something sacred.

Amy and the Eagle

At the time Amy's dad died and she first saw the eagle, she didn't remember all of her own past. But today, a mere month after her personal revelation, she knows the rest of the story. Amy is a Jewish, fortyish professional in the medical field and the mother of a two-year-old daughter. She lives with her Catholic husband, Rob, in Georgia. "Although it has its rough moments like any marriage, it's a good relationship," Amy said. "He's very stable and stoic and I'm very wild. I guess that makes a good combination!"

Amy and her husband lived on a lake for several years. When they first moved there, she saw bald eagles nest in a particular tree. However, by 1998, they hadn't seen the eagles in a number of years.

"My dad died, and when I came back from my dad's funeral, there was a young eagle near the house that I'd never seen before. My father's name was George, but his nickname in college was Eagle. When this eagle came, I just knew it was my dad. So whenever it showed up, I'd go out and sit there and talk to my father, George. This went on every day for quite a while, a couple of months at least."

Amy found it interesting that when she shared her story with friends, no one had any trouble believing it. A lot of them would say "Hey, I saw George today!"

Amy felt confident at this time that she had approached her father's death with all the tools and stability possible for a woman who for so many years had dealt therapeutically with parental issues.

"I got clean and sober twelve years ago and I made amends then. Basically I just worked through my problems. I was attending the twelve-step program and I included my father in everything I was doing."

Guilt was her biggest fear. After she left home as a young woman and throughout her life, George wrote letters that terrified her. "He would write letters about what a horrible daughter I was and that if he'd ever done such things to his father, he would never be able to live with himself. He kept repeating that I was going to feel guilty when he died. I was terrified my whole life that when he died, I would, in fact, feel eternally guilty."

When Amy first got the call that her father was very sick, she and her brother immediately drove to the town in which he lived. They got him to a doctor, he was hospitalized, and there they diagnosed him with incurable cancer. At the doctor's suggestion, George was placed in hospice care.

"I made two other trips to see him and stayed a week during one of those trips in a hospice house. I had to help him go to the bathroom and I slept in his room on a little cot. Every hour, on the hour, he would call out my name. 'Amy!' he would say in a croaky voice just to see if I was there. He was terrified of dying. He'd ask me to lie next to him on the bed and hug him and I did. Because I took the steps necessary to clean my life up, he knew that I loved him and I knew that he loved me. When he died, I did not have one ounce of guilt and it was a great reward. I knew that was because of the twelve-step program and the therapy that I had undergone."

But back when Amy was first beginning the twelve-step program, she was told by her therapist that she should sever the ties with her father because he was truly psychologically sick.

"I was raised Reformed Jewish," Amy explained. "We went to temple every Friday, I was bat mitzvahed and confirmed. I was also very active in temple as a kid. When we moved from the very cultural melting pot of New York to a very wealthy, Protestant area, we were the only Jewish family in our neighborhood. Eventually, we found a temple that was headed by a young rabbi who was terrific. I enjoyed it, maybe because I felt so different from everyone else in my neighborhood. It actually made me kind of cling to Judaism."

Amy hadn't seen that rabbi since she was seventeen. But when her father became ill, she located him. "He came to the hospice to see my dad; then he came back to do the funeral. And since then we've rekindled our relationship. He did our baby's naming ceremony; my husband and I visit him every year." Along with the appearance of the eagle, this reunion was a positive aspect of her father's illness and death.

Another reason she clung to her faith and activities at the temple was because life at home was not much fun. Amy's relationship with both parents was strained. "My father was very volatile verbally and my parents fought a lot. There was a lot of yelling in my house."

Amy imagines that when she was a little girl, she might have had a positive relationship with her dad, but she doesn't remember many good times. As she got older, the relationship was definitely unhealthy.

Although he never hit her, the verbal abuse and his emotional volatility were hard to live with. As Amy matured, she became more aware of his strangeness. Some of his actions were unlike those of most parents she knew. "I really think he was bipolar because he did such outrageous things," Amy said. "For instance, he used to lick my cheek. I'd push him away and tell him he was gross, but he kept doing it. He did it to my brother, too."

Amy has been in therapy off and on for many years. When one of her therapists mentioned that such a gesture often went along with parent-child molestation, and that the parent was establishing his territory, Amy simply thought that strange. She had no memories of molestation and continued to think of her father as simply bizarre.

George also had poor eating habits, which he passed on to his daughter. "My mother would always cook these really good, healthy meals for him, because he had gout and high blood pressure," Amy said. "He'd sit at the table and eat and then he'd say, 'Oh I'm so full,' and unbuckle his belt. Then an hour later he'd say, 'Come on, Amy, let's go,' and I always knew what that meant. We would either go to the mall and walk around the food court eating candy or pizza or something, or go to a convenience store and bring home a bunch of snacks. He was addicted to junk food. At the time, though, I didn't know such behavior wasn't normal."

It was only when Amy left home to go to college that she discovered how abnormal it was to sit in her room eating a half gallon of ice cream all by herself. "At first I couldn't understand why my roommates thought I was weird."

Food, however, was not the only addiction Amy developed. The day of her Bat Mitzvah, when she was twelve, was the first time she tasted alcohol. Neither of her parents drank. "They were handing champagne around the whole time," she remembers. "I have no idea how much I drank, but when I got home, I blacked out. I remember my mother waking me up for dinner. It was still light out and I thought it was the next day."

Amy began drinking heavily on occasion. By the time she was fifteen, she looked mature enough to get into bars and she began going to them regularly. Too often Amy woke up the next morning in the bed of a man she didn't know, with no memory of how she got there. At nineteen, she suffered alcohol poisoning, yet still didn't recognize that she had a problem. "I wasn't a daily drinker; I was a binge drinker, so I didn't realize that my drinking was a serious problem. I thought being an alcoholic meant you drank every day."

She continued to drink heavily for ten more years. "I would binge, throw up and black out," she recalled. "No matter what, I had to drink more than anyone else. My friends would tell me the next day that I had been a riot the night before. I'd ask them what I did, because I would have no clue. I'd completely blacked out. I drove drunk a lot and I thank God that, as far as I know, I never hurt anyone."

Amy has also struggled with her weight all her life. "I'm not obese, but I could lose thirty pounds," she said. "There's no question I'm addicted to food."

Even when she was an adult, her father continued his bizarre behavior. "I remember one time when my secretary came in and said that there was a gentleman to see me, but he wouldn't give his name. I knew instantly who it was; my heart started pounding and my hands got sweaty. I hadn't heard from him in a year, he lived halfway across the country from me, and there he was in my office. He expected me to drop everything and go to dinner with him. He had no boundaries."

Following her father's death, Amy saw an eagle near her home every day for several months. She felt it was easing her into a life with no father. But finally the bird stopped coming around. A little later, Amy and Rob adopted their first child, a brand new daughter.

One summer when her daughter was a year and a half, Amy enrolled her in swimming classes two towns away. Almost at once, an eagle showed up, perched near the swimming pool and remained for the entire lesson. At the next lesson, the same thing happened.

"I asked the swimming instructor if she'd ever seen that eagle before. She said she'd seen eagles in the area, but never had one come this close to the pool."

The swimming lesson was five days a week for ten minutes. "Every day when we showed up, the eagle would appear. According to the instructor, he never came around at any other time," Amy recounted. "I told the woman this story and said that the eagle was George, my father. After a while it got so that she would say, 'Hey, there's George. He's here again!' When we ended the lessons, the eagle never came back.

"I think my dad is watching over me and my daughter. He never knew my daughter, but I think he's looking out for her."

That winter, Amy and her family moved away from the lake so eagle viewing wasn't as likely. George the eagle simply became a pleasant memory. Life went on, but not smoothly. Amy and her husband were having problems and she could not sleep. "I blamed Rob for my problems," Amy said.

Amy first heard of Michael through a friend. Both she and her husband went to meet him. "I've been to many therapists," Amy said. "And I know quite a few in my professional field, but no one is like Michael. His approach is so unique." She and Rob committed to a year-long period of counseling with Michael.

"When Amy first came to me," Michael explained, "she was tense. Part of her life was based on denial, based on a narrow world with rules and secrets she had created in order to maintain the denial, and a deep-rooted fear of guilt. She unknowingly put memories in places where she wouldn't feel or see them. Whenever she grew weak, she would drink or go into episodes of excessive passion and drama. It came to the point where if she didn't heal, she would lose her husband and daughter and the dream of the family she'd finally achieved. She had something valuable enough to challenge her fear of guilt and her life of denial. With some psychotherapy and regressive work, she remembered incidents which had been locked away."

Amy could not believe what surfaced. "About a month ago, while in counseling with Michael, I remembered that my father molested me. I never knew it while he was alive. In fact, I'm grateful I never knew, because I don't think I could have handled confronting him. The memories were of when I was about five years old."

For a couple of weeks, Amy was in shock. The memory was a startling revelation, one that explained a number of lifelong sensations, confusions and habits. Amy now understood the basis of her life-long fear of guilt; it was the ultimate fear of finding out that the abuse was her fault.

"One day, I was driving to an appointment. I was on a back road and I saw a bald eagle hunkered down right in the middle of the lane, picking at some fast food containers that had been left in the road. I slowed the car down and managed to get very close to the eagle. I'd never seen one in the middle of the road like that. I was amazed, but until that moment, I didn't think of it in the context of my relationship with my dad! I slowly drove right up to this eagle and it just sat there, eating!" Amy sat quietly for a moment.

As she continued with her therapy, the pieces of her past came into place. Although her parents didn't drink, they had all the symptoms of addiction. Her father was addicted to food; her mother was addicted to her dogs and spent little time with Amy. Was it any surprise that Amy should have addiction problems herself?

Today, Amy and her husband are well on the road to healing. "I'm so grateful we met Michael," Amy said. "Since we have been working together I feel better about life, myself and my husband. We've been married for ten years, but sometimes it's a struggle. It was never a question of loving one another; it was a question of how to make it work. I asked Michael what a normal marriage is supposed to be like and he said there's no such thing," Amy laughed. "I truly feel that Michael is a gift from God."

"Amy's story is about an awakening," Michael said. "It's not necessary to believe that all the eagles she saw were the same bird. The eagle is a symbol of a certain kind of energy. And, every time an eagle shows up, it's significant.

"When the eagle came into her life prior to the memories resurfacing, Amy was already open to the idea of the eagle's significance. That was merciful in its own way. If this had happened while her father was still alive and she had no tools to deal with it, she surely would have gone back to alcohol and all her other symptoms of addiction.

"The eagle gave her an awareness of her father's presence and a sense of his value for her in a way she'd never recognized before. She began to look at life from a higher, more elevated perspective, albeit from a distance. Life became a little less personal and a little more universal. Amy's life had been very tightly wound because of her fears and her life-long suppression of guilt. Accepting the eagle allowed her to step back and take a more spiritual position, to actually let her have a sense of her own spirit existing outside of the situation and looking back at it all, like the eagle sitting on the branch.

"It was almost like her father was showing her, through the eagle, what it looks like to be back in the universe, not separate from it. It's not so big and threatening when we realize we're part of it."

The eagle in the road clearly showed Amy how her addictions were linked to her father, especially the one addiction which she had yet to conquer, food. Her father taught her to love eating junk and there was George the eagle eating trash thrown from a car. Amy laughed. "It doesn't get more clear-cut than that!"

An exciting aspect of this story is how closely linked Amy and Rob's experiences appeared to be. Both of them saw eagles in the middle of the road at about the same time. These eagles could not be avoided, and could not go unseen by them. This lesson was to be experienced, by both of them! The eagle on earth is very real, very connected, life at its most basic. The creatures weren't soaring far above the earth when Amy and Rob saw them, they were on the ground, also at risk.

"For Amy and Rob as a couple, it evidenced a connection between them to see eagles at about the same time," Michael continued. "I've been trying to get Rob to see that Amy's trauma, fear of guilt, and her defense mechanisms are very visible, while his are very obscure. Her trauma was more direct, while whatever happened to him in his youth was probably more subtle. Often, when two people fall in love, it's not a well person falling in love with a sick person. It's two people who may be equally wounded finding one another. The more similarities, the more exact the match. That's what I believe."

The owl, like the lofty eagle, is a difficult symbol to ignore, and has performed admirably as a spiritual guide.

June and the Owl

June grew up the older of two children, with a younger brother six years her junior. "When my brother was born, my whole life changed," June said. "Up to that point I had been an only child and the first grandchild." Life was good and she felt special. But her brother Jonathan was born with colic, and instantly the focus of the whole family changed.

"I was aware pretty early on that it was my responsibility as part of the family to help care for my brother, to protect him, make him happy," June recalled. By the time she was nine years old, her mother was forced to work outside of the home to help support the family. At that point, Jonathan was sent to stay with his grandparents, while his mother went to work and June went to school.

Her grandparents' home was a duplex with a common room between the two sections, both upstairs and downstairs. The grandparents lived on one side and leased the other side to another couple. Daily, the man who rented the other side of the house would come to fetch Jonathan and carry him upstairs where a pleasant sitting room was accessible from both houses, and where they were left alone.

"When I look back on it, I believe my grandmother must have known something was going on," June said. "In that era, of course, nobody discussed such things. They were denied or dealt with in passive-aggressive behavior. My grandmother was a gentle, quiet soul, yet she exhibited an intense dislike for the renters and, at times, quite differently from her normal behavior, was rude to them. She didn't want me ever going to their apartment. Of course, that only increased my curiosity and I would occasionally knock on their door and visit. I was always severely reprimanded for it."

When he finally entered school, Jonathan was no longer sent to his grandparents' house. Instead, June was expected to care for him after school and on Saturdays until her parents came home. Her brother grew up an unusually emotionally fragile child.

"I had to clean, cook and take care of Jonathan from a pretty early age," June recalled. "I became very performance oriented, seeking approval for the services I performed. I was expected to keep Jonathan safe and if he ever got into trouble or did anything disobedient, it was my fault and I was reprimanded severely for it. He was a hyperactive child and always into something so I was punished a lot."

As a teenager, Jonathan and his father were in constant conflict. June married at a very young age and moved away. When her brother was in high school, however, her parents called, begging June to take Jonathan to live with her and her husband. Of course, she agreed to take in her brother.

"In accordance with the family pattern, no explanation was given or discussion about what was wrong with Jonathan or why they wanted him to leave. I just knew that it was my duty to take care of him." It wasn't until later she learned that Jonathan's conflict with his father had intensified and that he had become involved with a homosexual man.

After a failed marriage and repeated bouts with alcoholism, Jonathan finally came out of the closet and began a homosexual lifestyle. Sadly, he became infected with the HIV virus. June fell into a deep depression despite her own wonderful life. In fact, her depression was partially because of her wonderful life. How could life be so good for her when her brother was dying?

It was only when her father died a few years ago that June had the stimulus she needed to seek help. She went into therapy with Michael, joining his weekly group sessions, and began working through some of her personal issues. "It was one of the most wonderful times of my life," she said. "I found a place where I felt safe, a place where inner feelings and fears could be shared. Gradually, over time, I was able to release my feelings of guilt for having had such a good life while my brother lived in misery. I was finally able to share the nightmares and thoughts that haunted me with Michael. I was consumed with guilt because I had not kept my brother safe from the man in the apartment. As illogical as it may sound to an adult's ear, this guilt infused my whole mind and body. There were times I was so depressed I felt I should end my life. I felt that I did not deserve a wonderful husband and children if my brother was unable to be happy and well."

As she began working some of this out in therapy, June also began taking long walks in the woods, which proved benifically thera-putically as well as physically. For the previous five years, she had lived in a wonderful, rural area in the midst of woods and pastures. She had already become tuned into nature and was appreciative of the lack of human noisome and polluting influence. Often, she would walk out in the evening and stand listening to the night sounds, the secret life of the nighttime woods.

Then one night, an owl appeared. It swooped low over her and landed in a nearby tree. The first appearance was a miracle in itself, but it continued to happen, more and more often. "I began to look for him every time I went out," June said. "I'd talk to him when he came near and he'd hoot back at me. Several times as I drove through the gate, the owl swooped down from a tree right in front of the car."

As June talked of the owl in her group therapy sessions, Michael invited her to look into its meaning. She learned of the owl's ancient mystery and its long association with wisdom and vision, and that it was representative of the ability to see into souls, know secrets, and appear at times of great change.

"One evening, my husband and I were in town in a nice residential neighborhood heading home from visiting friends. Suddenly, an owl flew down and landed right in the road, directly in front of the car. My husband had to step hard on the brakes and the owl continued to sit in the road, staring at me. I knew the owl had significance when it showed up in this neighborhood, which was an unnatural place for it to be. I knew it was trying to tell me something, but I didn't know what."

When she shared this experience with the group, Michael said, "June, the owl is trying to tell you something. If you don't get it soon, it might have to die to get its point across."

Later, Michael explained that had he thought, or tried to be protective or tactful, he never would have said such a thing. "I truly feel my blurting that out was inspired," he said. "But at the time, a minute after I said it, I wished I hadn't. June was already carrying a load of guilt around. We'd been working on this and talking about her misplaced guilt for quite some time, but she just wasn't getting it."

June tried to get it, but it was just out of reach. She dug deep, striving to understand her issues in wanting to help her brother, while at the same time resenting the pain he'd inflicted on the entire family. Still she felt the heavy responsibility of not having protected him when he was alive.

A week later, June came home to find her golden retriever acting strangely. "I followed him out to the garage and there on the dog's bed lay the owl, dead. It was almost more than I could bear; the pain in my heart was awful. My first thought was, 'Why didn't I save the owl? I didn't get its message quickly enough!'"

June fled to the group in agony. Weeping, she poured out her story and listened as the others began helping her process it. Suddenly, one sentence came through, loud and clear. "Michael had said this to me before, but I just hadn't heard it," she said. "Now I did. He told me that it was between the owl and God, that the owl had died because it was hit by lightning. There was absolutely nothing I could do to save it. I couldn't possibly keep an owl safe. That's completely beyond my realm of control.

"Suddenly, in my heart of hearts, I got it. I realized I had only been a child too. I could not have known what was happening to my brother, nor could I have protected him. I was only a child! And even today, I can't make him happy or well. It's outside the realm of my responsibility. I can only take care of me."

With blessed and sudden insight, June cried out, "There was nothing I could have done!" and burst into tears in Michael's arms.

"For the first time, I really knew I was okay," June said, her eyes welling with tears as she told the story. "It was the most liberating feeling I have ever experienced. I still can't tell the story without crying. I felt truly free to enjoy my own life for the first time.

"It's as if I had been encased in a curtain of darkness," she explained. "With the physical punishment I received every time my brother was hurt or in trouble, the lesson was literally pounded into me that I was responsible for everything that happened to him."

June went home and performed a ceremony with the dead owl, keeping a feather before burying the bird. She still feels sad that the owl died, but she also knows, every time she looks at the feather that the animal was a gift from God. The world became much brighter when she realized that someone cared for her so much.

"I have become very aware of God's creation by observing nature and his messages to me," she said. "But by far, the most impactful experience was with the owl. It is vivid in my memory because it went right to the very core of my being and became an instrument in setting me free from pain and guilt."

June did not see any owls for a long time after that. The day Charlene called her to talk about her story for this book, an owl landed near her barn gate then flew ahead of her from tree to tree up the lane before swooping away. A few days later, another appeared in the tree near her house. And at last, one swooped to a tree near where she was standing. She spoke to it and it flew to another tree, then landed on the ground where it stared solemnly up at her. This was the purest form of validation, not only for her, but also for the writers of this book.

"Women are the nurturers of our society," Michael said. "They take care of children, husbands, parents and jobs. They're expected to do so much. They're not the only ones that fall prey to guilt, but it seems more common for women to experience feelings of guilt.

"June had been meeting with me for some time, but she'd already discovered nature on her own. She was already open to the messages by the time she heard us talking about the concept. But she wasn't getting the one message she really needed.

"I told her God did not send her the owl so that she could take care of it. She was so accustomed to taking care of everyone. She'd been doing it all her life. But God sent this owl with a message. The owl came to set her free, to teach her that every life is responsible only for its own destiny. We have to learn to let our mothers, husbands, children live their own lives.

"June could only get the message when she was ready. She could only know what she knew. It was time for the owl, too. It didn't die just for her. The owl and June had come together in this scenario so that both of them could grow. Even the dog helped June! It was a really powerful lesson for me," Michael said.

"The truth is, if I feel guilty because my dog got loose and was run over in the street, I'm experiencing a delusion of grandeur," Michael said. "First off, yes, if I tied the knot better, my dog might not have gotten loose. However, the dog still didn't have to run out into the street, the driver didn't have to look the other way, the car didn't have to hit him. Those are things out of our control. It's between the dog and God. And when it's that dog's time to go, the knot will come loose!

"We have these excessive feelings of responsibility so that we can go to sleep at night and believe we are in control. We don't go to bed trusting in God's decisions, but we should."

We now turn to our beloved household animals, dogs and cats. It is not a coincidence that owls and cats should fall together in the same chapter. You may notice a clustering of animals around issues...that is how animal medicine first was observed and values established. It is not a coincidence.

Owls and cats are considered the most mysterious of animals, the consorts of witches and mediums. But while our society has turned some of this into a fear, the truth is that these animals are simply more aware of energetic fields: they are able to see things most of us have lost the ability to see. Both owls and cats have the ability to see in the dark, physically and metaphysically speaking. Both seem just a little closer to the world of spirit (than that of earth)...

Misty and the Cats

Misty, an attractive redheaded woman whose hair was touched with gray, had been seeing Michael for about a year, peeling layers of a very complicated psychological onion to determine the reasons for relationship failures, depression, and destructive, repetitive patterns in her life. Gradually, as she delved deeper, she became aware that at some time in her forgotten past she had probably been molested. Though the memories remained elusive, the feelings surfaced more and more.

In her struggles to learn about herself, she also embarked on a new spiritual journey, exploring Native American traditions and opening up to alternative ways of believing, healing and focusing her life. She was making a conscientious effort to live her life with greater awareness.

"In January of 1996," Misty began, "I committed to a Vision Quest the following summer. At the time I didn't realize that the quest really started on the day of the commitment, and it would last long after! Had I known what I was in for..." She shook her head, a wry smile on her lips.

A Vision Quest is a Native American ceremony that often marked a young man's rite of passage into manhood. Now, both genders and those of all cultures take part in quests, in order to grow and to find God and themselves. In a desert or on top of a mountain, somewhere where one can be alone in nature, an individual will fast and pray for three or four days, hoping to "see" something that will prove to be an important element in his or her future life.

Misty's preparation, under the tutelage of a Native American mentor, included reading her childhood diaries in order to recapture

lost energy still being spent in old and useless anger, resentment or misplaced blame.

"Every evening I read my own diaries, as my teacher suggested.
I was up to the time period when I was about twelve or thirteen. One
day, I was driving home from work when I suddenly had to pull off the
road and stop the car, because I was suffused with so much pain. I
remembered an incident that occurred when I was an early teenager
that had haunted me for a long time. It woke me in the night for many,
many years. Every time my mind landed on this memory, I'd quickly
push it away, just so I wouldn't feel the pain. Thankfully it faded as I
got older. Suddenly, on this day, the memory was back, just like in the
old days when I used to pray for this memory to be taken away from
me. It hurt so much; I hadn't thought of it in years."

As a young girl, Misty had lived on the midwestern grasslands.
One day, while reading a book outdoors, she gradually became aware of
a terrible noise. It was a cat, yowling. "My Siamese cat, Tan, was my
baby," she said. "He slept on the pillow by my head every night. I knew
as soon as I heard that yowl that it was Tan and that he was in trouble."
Tan had been badly injured by a roving pack of dogs just a few weeks
before, so instantly Misty knew what was happening.

By the time Misty raced to her cat, teetering on the top of a
metal, barbed wire fence post, it was too late. The pack of dogs surrounding Tan attacked him. Screaming, Misty dove through the pack
of dogs to snatch up her torn and bloody cat.

The memory haunted her for years. "I realized that I'd been
hearing the sounds of Tan howling for some time," she said. "But I was
so engrossed in my book that it didn't enter my consciousness until too
late. It nearly killed me to think that if I'd jumped up the minute I
heard the first sound, I might have saved him."

Over time, the memory stopped cropping up. Then suddenly,
driving in the car that day, it came back. It knocked the breath out of
me," Misty said. "I couldn't believe the memory of that awful day had
come back after all this time."

She managed to get the car back onto the road and drive home.
That evening, as she resumed her reading, she was not particularly surprised to read of Tan's death in the next section of her diary. Though

she had not thought of the incident in years, she'd been given a warning that she would experience it again. It was all she could do to get through it.

Misty had already scheduled a session with Michael. She mentioned the incident, casually thinking it ancient history. But when he asked her for details, she found she could not stop weeping. "We concentrated during the whole session on this memory," she said. "Michael took me back to that afternoon and I relived it again. When I came back to the house carrying my cat, I was screaming and crying, 'No, no!' My mother had come out and was trying to get me to stop screaming. She shook me and kept saying, 'What will the neighbors think?' I only realized then, with Michael, how angry I was at my mother and how awful a thing that had been. I'd never thought of it that way before.

"Michael encouraged me to scream it out now and promised he wouldn't shake or slap me. God, how I screamed. I felt so good!"

She also realized how angry she was at the dogs. "I wanted to kill them with my bare hands. In reenacting the experience and getting it out, Michael helped me reach an understanding that the dogs were just being dogs. And I was just being a little girl engrossed in a book. None of us could be blamed. I forgave the dogs and came out of that session feeling at peace, and far less guilty. Michael told me that I would perhaps still grieve, but the guilt wouldn't have the same power over me. He also told me that the guilt came from something deeper, something earlier than Tan's brutal death. But I wasn't able to reach back and connect it to anything else."

The day after her session with Michael, Misty went for a walk. She came to a house where a friendly, young, chocolate Labrador retriever bounded across the lawn to be petted. A cat was walking on the road ahead of her. Apparently, it had already passed the lab without exciting any attention, so Misty walked on without thinking much of the situation. But as she neared the cat, something didn't seem quite right. The cat kept a slow deliberate pace and looked neither right nor left as she came abreast of it.

"Of course, Tan was still fresh in my mind," Misty said, "so I was nervous about what that dog might do. Sure enough, it started bouncing and jumping and barking at the cat. I think the dog just wanted to play, but it still made me nervous."

Misty tried to chase it away, but the lab thought this was part of the game and wanted to include the cat. The cat stopped, unable to proceed past the barking, playful dog. By now, Misty realized something was wrong with the cat and picked it up.

"It obviously had a respiratory problem," she said. "I could hear the liquid sound in its breath. The animal was skin and bones, and yet it purred so loudly, I thought the purring might kill it. How could anybody let a cat get so sick?"

She saw the cat was part Siamese, just like Tan. Suddenly, she realized she was taking on the responsibility of protecting another cat from a dog. "Why?" she wondered. "I thought I was done with that work."

It was apparent that the cat was very sick. She put it down hoping it would go home, but it tried to follow her. Exasperated with the two animals, she picked the cat up, thinking she would carry it back to her place. "It seemed to be in pain, because it wouldn't stay still for long," she said. "Several times I put the cat down, hoping it would turn away and go home, but it kept following me."

Finally, she set the animal down and decided she would hurry home to get her car. The cat seemed to understand and sat in the middle of the road watching as she half walked, half ran back to her house. She worried all the way that a car would hit the cat and it would be her fault. When she finally ran up her driveway, it was dusk. Suddenly, a cat strolled across the drive, sat down and stared straight at her.

"I stopped short!" Misty said, laughing. "At first I thought it was the same cat and it was some kind of a spirit playing tricks on me. I'd never seen a cat at my place before. I guess because of the state of my mind just then, I was really shocked." As she approached the cat, however, she realized it was a young, gray, female and obviously pregnant. "When I got in my car to go for the other cat, I was starting to feel really weird. *What's going on with these cats?* I wondered."

Misty fed both cats that night, then took the sick one to the vet the next day. "It was really sick," she said. "I paid $60 of a $150 bill and the vet offered to cover the rest. We had to put the cat down. It was in terrible shape. I felt bad, but at the same time, I wondered if it had come to me in order to be put out of its misery. It was dying a slow, horrible death."

"Then my Vision Quest mentor, to whom I told this story, said something that really stopped me in my tracks," Misty said. "He asked, 'What if Tan, badly mauled from his first attack, had deliberately gone back to the dogs for the same reason?' Whoa, that put a whole new slant on things!"

Suddenly, death became a new issue for Misty. It had long been her belief that every soul picks its time and place when coming to Earth. Do we all choose to leave as well? Misty wasn't sure, but began to think she understood why the cats had come to her now, at this time of her search into her past to recapture lost energy.

"When one undertakes a Vision Quest, one dies to an old life in order to be reborn to a new one," Misty explained. "I had no idea the transformations I would undergo when I began the process, or the kinds of things about myself I would be forced to face."

Misty had made her intentions known by beginning her Vision Quest and the universe was responding. The cats, however, weren't finished with her.

"A friend of mine, who had never heard of Tan and didn't know what I was going through, called me one day in hysterics. Her pet, a healthy house cat, had escaped its confines and been torn apart by a pack of dogs. She ran, screaming from the house to try to rescue it and had even gotten ahold of it, only to have it torn from her hands again by the dogs."

Misty shook her head. "When I hung up the phone I was trembling all over. *What on earth had I started? Why a healthy house cat?* I didn't understand anything anymore."

And still it went on. A few days later, Misty was driving to work when a white cat darted from the side of the road in front of the car. She braked hard. "No!" she screamed as she saw it tumbling in her rear view mirror. She pulled to the side of the road. Fatally wounded, the cat had managed to get off the road and into the field to die. She knelt by it, sobbing and praying as the animal drew its last breath, thanking it for its life and apologizing for not understanding. *How many cats will die before I understand what the message is?* she asked herself. By now, it was clear to

Misty that the whole cat world was on a mission…a mission for her.

"I was scared to death that I was killing all these cats," Misty said. "I worked hard trying to understand what was going on. I was desperate to see that no more cats would die."

She studied. She questioned. She dug inside herself. She knew that cats were special spirits, more sensitive to energy than many animals. There was a reason why mediums and witches of storybooks are depicted as having cat familiars. Cats seem to know that the spirit is reality and to be far less attached to their bodies than other animals. Who has not felt the presence of a cat slip away, even while it physically remained?

"One day, my teacher and I were sitting outside my house talking. There was a family of wrens just around the corner from where we sat and the babies had just started jumping out of the nest to follow the parents around. While we spoke, I became vaguely aware of the presence of the gray cat, which had hung around my property since the first day she had shown up. I didn't like feeding her, because I knew that she kept birds and squirrels away, but how can you not feed a pregnant, homeless kitten, at least occasionally?

"I knew she was there looking for food, but I was so engrossed in our conversation that I ignored her. Suddenly, we both jumped at the sound of screeching. The gray cat had just grabbed one of the baby wrens," Misty said. "I love birds. If she'd caught a mouse, or even a squirrel, it wouldn't have had so much impact on me. I tried to chase her, but of course that was useless. I had to clap my hands over my ears so I couldn't hear the screeching. I felt so responsible. If only I'd fed her when she first came up, she wouldn't have taken the baby bird. I think that was when I really started to hate the sight of cats."

Some days later, Misty went to a Natural Awakenings workshop. The first evening, after arriving at the remote woodland area and unpacking her things, she stepped out of her room to see a scrawny white kitten slink around the corner of the cabin. She nearly dropped her bag. "I couldn't believe I was looking at a cat in the middle of so-called wilderness!" she said. "Even stranger, when I looked closer, I saw that it had one blue eye and one green eye."

During the workshop, Misty ended up in a place she had not

expected, working on her guilt about two abortions she'd had years earlier. By the end of her powerful sessions, she knew both peace and the purpose of the two little souls that had resided so briefly with her. She knew that those souls had chosen to come and to leave as certainly as she herself was on Earth. One green eyed, one blue-eyed. Once more, she now thought she understood the purpose of the cats.

As she drove home, (after being sure the white kitten had a new home with one of the other workshoppers) she reveled in her new freedom from a large portion of her long burden of guilt. She went back over the memories of many long dead animal friends, turning them loose to their own destiny for the first time.

"Many indigenous people have picked their own time to leave," she explained. "We have become removed from such a concept in our culture. For the first time, I realized that also must apply to animals." Gratefully, and certain that her trials were over, she offered thanks to the many cats that had worked with her that year, certain that it was over. The timing was perfect. It was time for her Vision Quest.

Misty headed out west to do her Quest, half afraid she would be pounced upon by a cougar. But while she had a powerful experience, no cats came to her. She had apparently learned her lesson.

She had many reasons to understand that the Vision Quest experience went on long before and long after the actual fasting in the desert. Shortly after her Quest, she opted to do another Natural Awakenings workshop. Although Misty was in a very good emotional place, she thought she was doing it to support a friend. "Everyone's heard that one before!" she laughed. "But I probably wouldn't have gone otherwise. So thank you to that friend!"

Much to her surprise, her experience at the workshop was again very powerful. "During the breathwork, not much happened for a while," she said. "Then, slowly, I realized I was an animal. I went a little deeper and discovered I was a cat!" A little surprised, Misty wasn't sure what to do with this until Michael, walking among the participants, came by and encouraged her to be the cat, to go all the way and feel it.

"I'd never felt anything like this before," Misty said. "I really became the cat. I was a female cougar. I could feel the languid movements of my body; I was sinuous, sensuous, and after moving and feeling and stretching, I realized I was making love!"

Misty went deeply into the whole experience of making love with a male cougar. Other workshop participants later attested to hearing a yowling sound such that some actually thought a cougar was present. From there, however, still under the close supervision of the therapists, Misty began to realize she was a little girl, on her back on a kitchen floor, legs in the air.

"It felt so bizarre. But a vague memory had actually come back. I realized what was happening and at first I was scared and embarrassed. But the therapists encouraged me to continue feeling, not to place rational constraints on it. As I gave in to reliving the experience, I realized that I liked it!"

Misty still does not know who it was that was with her. But one more layer of her psychic onion had been peeled away. By the middle of the session, she realized where a lifetime of guilt had come from. "I liked it," she said. "Whoever it was that did that to a little girl, what I carried with me the rest of my life and felt the guiltiest about, was that I liked it."

" 'Of course,' all the therapists said, 'Why not? If it feels good, why shouldn't you?' That, however, is not what you feel when you're young and some part of you thinks you're bad. When I returned from reliving that experience and stood up," she went on, "I was a woman, not a helpless child. For the first time in my life, I didn't feel victimized at all. I had liked what happened to me and I was no more responsible for that than I was for the fact that it happened!"

Never had Misty felt so light, so free. The feeling of being a sensuous cat stayed with her to such a degree that when the group broke up, she went into the woods alone, walking with light step, breathing in fresh, tangy air. "I was still feeling like a cat," she laughed. "That kind of feeling doesn't happen often, so I just gave in and enjoyed it again. I crawled up a boulder, feeling the smooth muscles in all my limbs, and sank down in cat position to look down the sloping hill. I felt I could lick my whiskers; I felt the warmth of the sun-baked rock. When I gazed down the slope, I knew that I would never feel the same sense of guilt again."

"Misty's was one of the more complex problems we deal with," Michael said. "We have lots of abused people who come in and work through their issues. But I've often found that when things are so deeply buried that even after lots of work, memories haven't returned and when the guilt is as strong as it was here, it can be because the guilt is about liking what happened to them. Well, if pain isn't involved and something feels good, why not? But we think our society will frown on us for that.

"In this case the guilt and the memory were so buried, in fact still are to some degree, that she had to become a cat to get there at all. She couldn't be herself."

In fact, Misty had to turn into her own animal angel in order to be healed and relieved of the burden of guilt that she had carried for so long. As in the stories of Melinda, Amy and June, it was though the intercession of animal angels—spiders, eagles, owls and in Misty's case, cats, that guilt, retrieved from the past was recognized for what it was, and banished.

chapter four

Depression

Some men fish all their lives
without knowing it is not fish they are after.
—*Henry Thoreau,* Journal

Although clinical depression has many causes and effects, Michael has long held to the belief that depression results from the suppression of and emotion, though predominately anger. Frequently, anger is squelched and concealed within, because our society teaches people that anger is bad. Few of us have training in how to deal with this emotion effectively, so we often don't handle it well and we fear it. We have internal permission, however, to induce rage upon ourselves. The invective we'd like to shout at someone else is turned on ourselves.

"We suppress anger because we don't know what the rules of anger are," Michael explains. "The first rule: Anger, when expressed in the moment, is a beautiful, clear, pure source of energy to make something happen. But we swallow it most of the time, and it sours and grows in our stomachs, so that when some of the anger eventually escapes, long after the fact, we overreact and spew venomous words at the person who happens to be pushing our buttons at the time.

"The second rule: The *appropriate* use of anger is to employ the energy that comes from it and use it to become determined to make our own lives better. Determination is the word we use for well-focused anger."

When depressed, we often abuse ourselves. "Even if all we're doing is suppressing the energy of our anger and we haven't gone so far as to say 'I hate myself,' the festering emotion still becomes bitterness inside," Michael said.

Depression has become pervasive in our society, and is the most frequently cited reason individuals seek psychotropic medication. Yet, because it is not a real emotion, but rather the suppression of real emotions, it can be extremely difficult to overcome. Many of us suffer some level of depression at some point in our lives.

In 1996, when Charlene went off into the woods to live in her shed, her heart and soul were in such pain that it felt like a constant, deep, bone ache. She could hardly relate to anyone, because she had truly became a hermit. She had a special encounter, though, that enabled her to go on for just one more day. Sometimes, that is all that we can ask. Sometimes, that is all that is necessary; sometimes, that is all that is possible, taking life one day at a time.

She had been avoiding her closest friends, her sailing buddies, because they reminded Charlene of her beloved partner, whom she had left behind. However, she found sailing was therapeutic, so one day she went out on the lake with a couple of friends. As they tacked across the lake, two dragonflies suddenly appeared in the air, joined together. They hovered a moment, looking for a place to land. Without thinking, she raised my finger and instantly they alighted.

Charlene moved to the lower side of the boat where the wind was less strong and sat there for the next half hour while the two dragonflies mated on her finger. One was red; one was green, but that was not the awesome part. She said, "At a time in my life when I was depressed, and felt the most alone and the most unloved I'd ever felt, I learned something new about the animal world. I had never realized that when dragonflies mate, they form a heart.

"For half an hour I stared at a red and green heart, perched on my finger in two unmistakable symbols of love, the mating act itself, and the shape of the heart. For that half hour at least, my depression lifted; I felt loved."

Dragonflies are associated with light and water. Water often represents emotions. The neglect of emotions is something the dragonfly brings to our awareness. And of course, both light and water, when broken into prisms, are about color. Keeping color and emotions alive is very important. Dragonflies remind us that we are light and can reflect light in a powerful way. They represent the divine brightness of transformation. They are about awareness and lifting burdens.

Jessie and the Dragonflies

Jessie is a lovely, serene-faced woman who has struggled with clinical depression, to the point of taking a variety of medications, most of her adult life. She is a businesswoman living with her husband in the South on a beautiful wooded acre of land, upon which she has carefully nurtured native plants. The result is a wonderful backyard natural habitat, which is water- and soil-efficient in the middle of an otherwise "traditional" residential area. Birds, butterflies and most of the insect world, as well as the occasional snake, raccoon, or other such woodland creatures, call this tiny corner of the world home, thanks to Jessie's careful and conscientious tending.

She gets back as much as she gives from this healing habitat, particularly from one small creature. "I know that dragonflies are my special totem," she said, "and that they're a totem of luck, happiness and tranquility. But this has been a year of more healing and peace than I've ever known and, sure enough, dragonflies seem to be everywhere. I have special encounters with them every time I walk out into my yard."

Early in 2002, taking the advice of a concerned friend, Jessie went to Michael for counseling. Depression was again rearing its ugly head. Two ongoing issues in her life had begun to affect her once more, her continuing trouble with her husband and longtime struggles with work. Michael helped her burrow deeper into the source of her depression. Some revelations she was ready for, some, she was not. Jessie would never again be able to not know the things she discovered through this counseling, whether she chose to deal with them head-on or not. In some ways, just the awareness seemed to be enough for her.

Slowly, she began assimilating the new knowledge into her life. As she did, she became more and more aware of the presence of dragonflies, which seemed to add a dimension of connection and tranquility to her life.

It was in the spring following her counseling sessions with Michael when she first began to notice dragonflies. A few years earlier, Jessie and her husband had decided to get into kayaking, something neither of them had much experience with. At first, skills and techniques came slowly, especially since Jessie's husband, Craig, wasn't anywhere near as interested in the sport as she was. But it seemed that in the past year and a half, it had all been coming together, and Jessie felt her kayaking skills were soaring to a new level.

"Craig and I went for a long, overnight kayaking trip for the first time this spring. At the start, we were having a lot of problems and were pretty nervous. A couple of things broke and we had trouble getting the packs to stay put. Just as we resolved the problems, a dragonfly came and perched on my life preserver. It stayed with me throughout the first day of the trip, which was a pretty long first day. Well, Craig and I had a great time. Even with all the early problems, we reached our destination before nightfall."

"I don't know why, but as we finished setting up camp, thoughts of my mother popped into my head. It felt like her presence had been with me the whole way through."

Although it was the first time a dragonfly was that relentless about being noticed, it has not been the last. It seems that every time Jessie gets into her kayak now, a dragonfly appears, and along with the dragonfly come thoughts of her mother.

"I have always had a lot of angst about my mom," Jessie said. "You never really know your parents as adults unless you have the opportunity to experience them and relate to them as adults. My mom died young, so all I know is what she meant to me as a child. And it wasn't good."

Jessie moved to Georgia with her parents and a much older sister when she was about eight years old. By the age of twelve, with her adult sister ready to leave the house, Jessie became the main caregiver for her mother, who had such a host of physical and mental ailments that she could no longer function. Jessie remembers nothing pleasant or fun about her childhood. This had contributed enormously to her depression as an adult. It wasn't until her father died and she and her sister began going through picture albums that she began to glean some understanding of who and what her mom really was.

"You just don't think about your parents as individuals, or in any way other than how they parented you. Who they were when they were young or what their dreams might have been or what gave them pleasure were questions I never asked before. My mother grew up in the city and left to run a YWCA camp in the country. I think she was more of an intellectual bohemian than I ever realized.

"When she was up north, she loved the outdoors and the water. She passed that on to me. I saw pictures of my mom on the waterfront, canoeing, and I started to see the young woman who existed before all the disappointments of life caught up with her. She was a camp director for forty-five years and she loved nature.

"I knew all these things before, but it never registered with me. When I knew her as my mother, she was a hardened, sad person, totally in denial. She had many physical problems, which I think were the result of her great unhappiness and frustration. Her emotional despair manifested itself physically.

"When she came to Georgia, she gave up her whole support system. She left behind her camp co-workers, her relatives and her entire social connection. It didn't help that my dad was a traveling salesman and was gone all week long. She didn't like it down south, because it was so different from where she grew up. It was too hot, humid and buggy for her, especially with the particular physical ailments she had. She gave up everything that was once meaningful to her. For the most part, I knew my mom as a person who gave up and lost all hope. That was my reality. She was a bitter woman who was always ill and complaining about my father not living up to her expectations."

However, with the dragonflies spurring memories of her mother, Jessie's perspective concerning her mom has taken a new turn.

"More and more I'm aware of the young person my mom must have been, the athletic woman and the nature-lover. She also loved science as it related to nature and she had a connection with the water. We certainly share the connection with water and the outdoors.

"I'm beginning to realize that my mother was a pretty neat individual before I knew her. Little by little people have given me information and told me stories about her. Now when I'm on the water, it's almost like her presence is with me. I feel in tune with her love of the water, and connected to one-ness, that now-ness, the serenity of it. I think I've got a new link to my mother—one that I never had before. All the angst and anger I felt toward her seem to be slipping away. It's too bad you can't heal such things before it's too late." She was silent a moment. "But then, maybe it's never too late."

Throughout the summer, dragonflies seemed to be everywhere for Jessie. "My awareness is so tuned in to them these days," she said. "My mom and my healing are a big part of it, but that's not all."

As Jessie learned more about her mother, she was confronted with the shocking realization that she shared many of her mom's attributes and tendencies. Some were a little tough to recognize, still others were uncannily parallel to her own life. "My mother was more educated than my father and I think she always resented the fact that she didn't have a suitable intellectual partner to share ideas with, which is a parallel in my own life. She blamed my dad for everything and I've been blaming Craig for all my problems and thinking that he isn't supportive. I've finally realized this year that he is, in fact, very supportive. I hadn't given myself permission to take care of myself. I wanted to blame him, but it was really about me not wanting to take the risks. So I've been taking those risks, trying to find the balance between being in a relationship and having my own needs met. Being in a relationship means recognizing that the other person can't always be everything to you all the time."

Jessie feels that many of her past wounds are healing. "It has a lot to do with the dragonflies, with doing more of what defines me as a person. Somehow these little creatures play into my awareness and my centering."

Now, whenever things get bad, Jessie does a dragonfly meditation that she invented. She's very aware that when she meditates, it's about letting go of anger, frustration and the things that used to oppress her. She explained the meditation, saying, "When I'm stressed out from work or from a problem with my husband or something, I go into my yard and I sit down in the grass. I watch and I wait for a dragonfly to come into my field of vision. When one comes by, I concentrate on the dragonfly, but then I also concentrate on the aspect of nature and beauty in which it exists. I just sit and watch that dragonfly and assign it a particular burden. When another dragonfly comes into the picture, I refocus on that one and when I later think to look for the first one, I realize it's gone and whatever anxiety or burden it was assigned is also gone."

Even her stresses about work are now alleviated by this form of meditation.

"If I'm at work in the morning and I start to feel stress or anxiety, I'll use the excuse of checking the mail or simply step outside and stand there till I get my dragonfly quota. I'll just stand there and wait. You can almost tell by the temperature of the day how many will appear. I'll say, okay, because it's on the cool side today, I can only expect to see three. I'll stand there and spend that amount of time waiting for my three. Then I hate to go, because I want more. But I do set my quota. On warmer days, they're everywhere."

Whenever Jessie finishes a meditation or fills a dragonfly quota, she is left with a sense of tranquility and peace. "It takes me out of the daily grind and gives me a moment where I can refocus and rise above the everyday minutia. Actually, what it is more than anything is transcending work-a-day or relationship problems."

"I've seen so many different kinds of dragonflies this year. Maybe, it's my highly tuned awareness, but in the past I've never seen more than one or two types before. But this year I've seen so many. For example, the little short golden-bodied ones, Amberwings, or the ones I call bombardiers, that I thought had pouches like a bumblebee's, but it's actually part of their wing. I've seen red ones; long, pretty green ones; and short, stubby blue ones.

"I had the most delightful encounter right in my front yard last evening," she said. "I was walking around the yard, enjoying the coolness of the evening, watching butterflies and taking a native plant inventory—just checking on my treasured volunteer flora. As I approached a particular bush in my yard, I was aware of dozens of dragonflies flitting around the bush. As I got closer, I was aware of flutter-ing noises by my ear and I could feel the most delicate pressure. There had to have been two dozen dragonflies working this bush, in and out, up and down. They never actually landed but they brushed past me.

"I must have stood there for fifteen minutes just letting them glide over me. It was such a delight. I could barely see them as the day-light dwindled, but I could feel them brush by and hear their gos-samer wings. I was so mesmerized that I didn't want to leave their company. I finally had to force myself to leave. I realized I had told Craig I was just going down to get the mail and he was waiting for me.

She went back to get Craig and took him down to the bush. Of course, no one is ever as enamored of a special experience as the person to whom it happened, but that was okay with Jessie.

"Things have actually been pretty good lately. I think it's because I've taken the reins of my life back a bit and I'm honoring my needs. Really it's not that much. I was in this great turmoil at the begin-ning of the year, but along the way it just kind of healed itself. Not totally, though, there will always be longings, but I've done more to honor my needs.

"I think some of it's about acceptance. I feel more settled. I'm not stressing about the fact I am in my late forties, and am experienc-ing changes which connote aging in my body. I'm just like, 'Eh, oh well.' I went to an eye exam and found out that had to get a new pair of glasses. I looked in the mirror and saw my dad. I haven't escaped him either," she laughs.

"I'm not quite sure what significance dragonflies hold for me, but I know I feel such a great sense of tranquility and strength in their presence. When I think about the things that used to bother me, the bad thoughts don't have the significance that they used to have. They don't have the bite anymore. And anytime a dragonfly happens to grace me by landing on me, my endeavors seem to turn out favorably."

"Jessie was most certainly a black and white thinker," Michael said. "She had even been diagnosed as bipolar. A doctor may diagnose someone as bipolar. However, such diagnoses, though made by profes-sionals, do not always tell the whole story, nor do they do more than transfer information. They offer little in the way of the color or shadings that truly characterize the individual, only the extremes of the definition.

"The rainbow of color that now has entered Jessie's life is about the exciting range of potential emotional experiences to which she is now open. The dragonfly is the perfect animal symbol for her to choose. It brought to her an idea of a new exciting way to live, a way to become more flexible. Her acceptance of this, and her turning toward it every time she becomes overburdened works more effectively than any pill. At some point, she may have needed to take drugs to get here, to hear this message, but now, she doesn't need medication."

Jessie also is a prime example of how one can take one's totem, or animal guide, and use it effectively as a tool for overcoming life's daily stresses.

Like the dragonfly, which brings awareness and lifts burdens so that one can heal, cats have long been associated with healing. Cats symbolize surviving in the world; we've all heard that cats have nine lives. Sometimes, when struggling with the most basic issue of survival, the cat that appears or exists in one's life may be the symbol of living on despite everything. Cats represent independence, but sometimes, only by being dependent do we learn independence.

CJ and KitKat

CJ has an unusual profession. She is a joy meister. She teaches people how to live joyfully. But today, while she considers that career her life mission, she fully recognizes that she has struggled most of her life to find the joy in her own path. Severe depression and several suicide attempts are CJ's history, as are a number of major accidents, which could have easily fulfilled her suicidal wishes, but didn't.

She credits her partner for being a large part of the reason why she is not only alive today, but joyful, healthy and teaching others how to be the same.

In 1997, CJ first visited and then moved to the western United States in order to be near her disabled and failing mother. CJ herself was not in good shape after three debilitating car accidents from the year before, which caused brain injuries, and finally, a nervous breakdown. CJ and her mother both needed care.

"Mom wanted to adopt a cat," CJ said. "We talked about what kind of cat would be appropriate for her and I suggested that due to her limited mobility, she might want an older, more stable cat that would not race out the door every time Mom opened it. So we called the humane society and they said they did have an older female. Well, when we went, it was love at first sight for both of us, but, of course, this was to be mom's cat. So she adopted this cat and named her Kat in honor of my niece, whose name is Katherine."

Kat is a gorgeous tortoishell with large, seafoam green eyes, the first thing people tend to notice. "One of the vets who later treated her said that she looks like she couldn't decide what color to be, so she picked them all." CJ laughed, and said, "She's got stripes on her tail and spots on her legs and four different colors. She has very long whiskers that make me sometimes call her Catfish Face. And she looks like she's wearing black lipliner."

After Kat had lived with CJ's mother a few months, her mother informed CJ that something was wrong with Kat's ear. Sure enough, CJ discovered a terrible infection. "Kat's illness was beyond my mother's ability to cope with. The ear had to be cleaned twice every day; it was an awful infection. I took the cat to the vet weekly. Mom had only had her about four months, but it got to the point where it was hard on me to have to come over every day and do all this, so I suggested I'd just keep her until we got it cleared up. It never did clear up. So my mother told people I had stolen her."

CJ was going through a very dark period. "This was my dark night of the soul," she admits. "It took several years for me to really get through it, but KitKat's been there with me all the way through. Caring for her gave me something to live for. At the time, though, it was pretty touch and go for me."

CJ spiraled downward through the next year and a half. At her most desperate ebb, she attempted suicide. The pain in her body and the pain in her heart were more than she could bear. In the midst of this, CJ's mother passed on and Kat truly became CJ's animal. CJ felt a strong psychic connection with the tortoiseshell, and shortly after truly gaining ownership, Kat let CJ know that she wanted to be called KitKat, which is a double recognition of the name Katherine. Now, CJ truly had another consideration besides her own health. KitKat continued to insist upon attention. The infection simply would not go away. In fact, it got far worse.

"Finally, the veterinarian did surgery," CJ said. "In the process, he accidentally nicked the optic nerve, which damaged KitKat's right eye's ability to close completely. But it seemed to clear up the ear at last."

CJ and KitKat then moved to Florida. Almost immediately the ear infection flared up again. "I took her to a surgical unit; they did X-rays and removed the ear canal. It required having the ear opened permanently. Again, everything seemed to be taken care of."

CJ and KitKat were living in a basement apartment that had a high percentage of moisture, which created mold and mildew on everything. CJ was constantly concerned about her own health and KitKat's well being. She was not happy and kept looking for another place to live. A new home, with her limited finances, however, simply did not materialize.

"Then KitKat developed a constant upper respiratory problem, sneezing and wheezing and all," CJ went on. "I took her to an acupuncture vet and started her on acupuncture, chiropractic procedures and Chinese herbs. She'd already been on a natural raw foods diet but we started being more proactive with it."

The acupuncturist asked to see the X-rays. The surgeon sent them to her, and she showed them to CJ. "She asked me if I knew the cat had been shot with a BB gun," CJ said. "She had a pellet lodged inside the brain cavity and either no one saw it or no one bothered to tell me about it. The speculation is that it entered through that ear and that was what had caused all the problems. And all the problems from the ear canal weakened her immune system so that she's now susceptible to upper respiratory infections."

About the same time, CJ was consulting a spiritual astrologist seeking guidance on a new home, new career and new health. "She said KitKat was trying to teach me something," CJ said. "I've thought a lot about it and now, when I look back, a lot of things became clearer."

KitKat came into CJ's life at a time when CJ's health was poor. Instantly KitKat's health turned bad. CJ had suffered a brain injury, the result of a serious trauma. KitKat had been shot, also a serious trauma, and a pellet was lodged permanently in her brain. The pattern was becoming clear. Perhaps one of the greatest gifts KitKat brought to CJ was a focus outside of herself. Despite such serious depression that she had considered suicide, CJ worried about something else that needed her care.

"You could say that she gave me a reason to keep on living," CJ admitted thoughtfully. "Her ongoing presence in my life has been a tremendous healing experience."

When it was pointed out that many people would have considered such labor-intensive care a major pain in the neck, and possibly even put the cat down, CJ says she never even considered such a thing. "Focusing on her was a big way for me to get through my own problems. I can't imagine what my life would have been like without her."

KitKat also helped CJ find two new careers. As CJ healed, she turned to doling out joy as a part of her own healing. She had long been interested in alternative healing and metaphysical beliefs. Then, stumbling onto the excellent veterinary acupuncturist turned out to be a far more important discovery than CJ could have guessed. "It was a great gift to find a person who treated animals that way, and I've told many people about her since. Then I took the next step. It was a major 'ah hah!' "

CJ had been practicing Bach Flower Essences for twenty years. She had helped many friends with her knowledge. Suddenly, after seeing an acupuncturist work with animals, she realized that she could use Flower Essences for animals too. "I'd never even thought of giving them to KitKat!"

Bach Flower Essences is a procedure in which the essences of specific flowers or grasses are boiled down into a strong concentrate and fermented in alcohol. This process was invented some 150 years ago in England by a man named Bach. The idea is that the essence of the flower is preserved and is taken, a drop at a time, under the tongue. It is subtle "medicine" but is very powerful for those who can tune into its subtlety.

Immediately, she put KitKat on a regimen of Flower Essences. She also began a Flower Essence therapy business focusing mostly on the animals. "I've been able to help a lot of people with their animals, although I still work with people too!"

"As for KitKat, the vet said she'd have to be on those Chinese herbs the rest of her life. I had to give them to her through a syringe in her mouth twice a day. She was good about it, but it was so time consuming. She's off them completely now and she's doing very well."

In CJ's words, both KitKat, who is now twelve years old, and CJ are, "vital and radiantly healthy. I've had lots of animals in my time, but KitKat's...I can't even explain what she's been to me. She's my guide and I don't question the idea that she's an angelic presence in my life. She evokes so much joy in me, and I draw on that joy daily to assist me in every aspect of my life.

"We're partners. We healed together. I always tell her what's going on and let her know the options."

"This is a really wonderful story. I would say KitKat has changed CJ's attitude about living," Michael said. "It's the kind of story that enlightens me, it lifts my life up just hearing this story!

"I've become aware over the years that in some cases our children and our pets manifest the diseases we ourselves have, and that somehow or other they become so linked with us that our energy field influences theirs and vice versa. This concept is simple physics, so this is nothing far out or wild. This exchange of energy is like a person is projecting onto an animal in order to learn how to heal. That's what CJ did with KitKat. I believe this is where God gets involved. Not only did CJ have a cat, she had a cat with latent brain damage that showed its influence constantly. This is a reminder to me that there are universal mysteries bigger than any of us and we will never understand it all."

Cats represent mystery as well as healing, and KitKat was certainly a mysterious force. CJ wasn't paying attention to her own magic, her own ability to heal. Like the shoemaker's kids with holes in their boots or the mechanic who never has time to fix his own car, CJ had a skill that she had never thought to apply. KitKat helped her realize that she could heal herself with her own God-given beliefs and skills.

Annie and Kippy

Annie is a woman who has suffered with and fought depression on and off all of her life. But throughout the years, when she would be in the worst of her depressions, she always had one thing that kept her going on, one thing that kept her from sinking to the ultimate depths, from which some people never return. An experience from childhood remained so powerful to her all the way into her later years that she never doubted that she was here for a reason, and that the fight to live was worth it.

In the fifties, Annie was just like any other happy little girl. "We were a postcard-perfect family in those days," Annie said. "We had a red brick house in Ohio with a yard a block long and a creek in the back. I had two older sisters, Mom and Dad and Kippy."

Kippy was a pure white collie that their grandfather had bred and given to Annie several years earlier. The dog had already been a comfort to Annie's mother during the death of her parents and was a very special member of the family.

Annie's mother, Ella, would later remember that year as one of the worst times of her life. One day Annie, then five years old, was playing with Kippy in their back yard; the next day she was whimpering about a painful mouth, then a sudden fever took hold of her. Ella quickly called for a cab to take them to the hospital. By the time the cab arrived, Annie's skin had begun to peel. Within hours of the first symptoms, Annie was in the hospital, deathly ill, and the doctors had no idea of what was wrong.

At that time, parents were allowed to visit their hospitalized child for only one hour, three times a day. "My mother told me that not being allowed to stay with me was the worst," Annie said, "that and the fact that the doctors didn't know what was wrong. Her little girl seemed to be dying and everything they did made things worse."

Years later, they would assign a technical name to Annie's disease, but at that time, the doctors didn't know what they were dealing with and simply struggled to keep the little girl alive.

Annie was in the hospital for ten days. For several of those days her fever stayed well above one hundred degrees fahrenheit. She was delirious and her skin peeled as though she had second degree burns over most of her body. Despite the restrictions, Annie's parents managed to spend most of those first days in the hospital. But finally the night came when the doctor sent them home. "He told my parents that my fever would either break that night or they would lose me. He promised to call when there was any change."

As an adult, Annie remembers that night very well, though as a child, she had no point of reference by which she could understand the experience. "What I remember, as clear as yesterday, was that I just couldn't stay in my body any longer. It was too much work. I had what felt like a vision or a dream or something. I was running across an endless green plain like our back yard, laughing and full of life. I was chasing a white light. But then, the white light turned into Kippy. She stopped, turned around, sat down and looked right at me. There weren't any real words, but plain as day, she told me to go back home, because my family needed me. Then she got up and trotted off."

Just then, the nurses lowered Annie into a cool oatmeal bath. The shock and relief of her burning body being lowered into that bath was the first lucid moment Annie had experienced since slipping into delirium.

It would be many years later, after Annie began to hear stories of people who had died clinically and come back to life, that she finally had some means of explaining her experience. "Their stories were so familiar to me," she explained. "Their floating above their own bodies; the white light they seemed to follow; there always seemed to be the face of Jesus or Buddha or a loved one. It took a while to realize that this was what I had experienced."

That same night, Annie's parents had gone home in shock from the doctor's words about their daughter. As they entered the back yard from the garage, they found Kippy lying sick in the grass. Already grieving over the uncertain future of their beloved daughter, this was almost more than they could bear. Tenderly, they carried Kippy inside, then sat together on the landing between the kitchen and basement with the dog in their arms. They wept as Kippy died.

At that very instant, the phone rang. "It was the hospital," Annie said, even today unable to hold back the tears. "They told my parents that the fever had broken and their daughter would live.

"Dad taught Sunday school when I was a kid," Annie went on. "He had a simple and consistent message that 'God is love,' but he seldom spoke of religious or spiritual matters on a personal level. The one time we talked about my being so sick when I was little, he said, 'The dog died so you could live.' It was a simple, immutable fact to him." Later, when Annie studied Native American concepts, her father took the dog as his special totem.

Recovery for Annie, however, was not instantaneous. She suffered memory loss after her illness. "As I began to heal, I had to be reintroduced to the world," she explained. "Only because my mother sat beside me for hours before I was lucid, saying over and over again, 'It's Mommy, I'm here,' did I know who she was. Then I had to be reintroduced to my dad. And a couple of days before I was supposed to go home, I asked Mom to bring me a picture of my sisters, so I would know who they were when I saw them."

Annie remembers that picture well. It was taken in the back yard and showed her two sisters with Kippy on the bright green lawn. At last the day arrived when she was well enough to go home. "They were going to take me in through the front door, but I fussed until they took me to the back. I still remember the hurt and confusion I felt because Kippy wasn't there."

There was much more healing to be done. Going back to Kindergarten was hard. "Everybody knew me, but they were strangers. I just watched and did what they did. I didn't remember anything." But she would never forget a white collie frolicking on a vast green lawn and telling her to go home.

"These events fundamentally affected who I am today," she said, wiping her tears. "I dreamed and drew and wrote of the white dog for many years. She is a symbol of sacrifice to me, of purity of purpose and acting on intentions. She told me that there was purpose to my life. Whenever I experience depression, I try to focus on Kippy, who told me my life had purpose. Today, I treasure life and people and being of service...and I am committed to the animals of the planet."

"If I hadn't heard these kinds of stories a number of times," Michael said, "I'd have a hard time believing them myself. But the people who have these experiences simply cannot be talked out of them. The experience is very real, very strong for them.

"When we talk about depression, it's about a person turning

against himself or herself. We have no permission to send our angry energy outside of ourselves, so some other source has to come into our lives for us to heal, because we can't do it ourselves. With Annie, it was almost spontaneous combustion. There was so much heat, so much energy within her she almost ignited."

One way of absorbing such a story is to understand that Annie was shown the way. If we believe all energy is finite and is only an exchange, then Annie was shown something early in life. As her dog suffered that she might live, so perhaps she now suffers so that another might live. It is the Christ story repeated in her own life.

"Again, it's Newtonian physics," Michael said. "For every action there has to be an equal and opposite reaction. For some people to have good lives, others will suffer. Annie's sense of joy may only come through what happens with others. This is a major reason for dedication to others. I used to think such people were being martyrs. Today, even as recently as my last workshop, I've been shown that this isn't necessarily true. It's about the balance in the universe. When such people can accept this condition, that their joy comes through others, they will actually be able to experience joy for themselves. Annie can bask in the knowledge that the suffering in her life has brought less burden to others. She, like Kippy, is the hero."

chapter five

Anger

I was angry with my friend,
I told my wrath, my wrath did end.
I was angry with my foe,
I told it not, my wrath did grow.
                    —*William Blake*

"Anger is an emotion we get hung up on in our culture. We believe that it is negative," Michael explained. "From childhood we are taught to suppress our anger, taught that we are bad children when we get angry. We're punished for it. By the time we are adults, most of us have been suppressing so much anger for so long that it comes out in deleterious ways that affect our health, relationships, lives."

Suppressed anger has been scientifically proven to cause elevated hormone levels which can lead to type-two diabetes and heart problems in adults. Therefore, learning appropriate outlets for anger can lead to improved health. The truth is, anger is just another emotion, another form of energy.

Like most emotions, anger has its appropriate place. Frequently, anger is about boundaries being violated. Warnings of such feelings would be appropriate, but may not be given. When we suppress our anger, or even refuse to acknowledge it and don't give any warnings about violated boundaries, then our emotional burden builds as we suppress our feelings only to explode at an inappropriate time, and we end up hurting someone. It needn't be that way.

"Think of how animals show their anger," Michael suggested. "Roosters strut, bulls paw the earth, dogs scratch with their hind legs, owls change their call. Something violates their boundaries and they use anger appropriately, to maintain those boundaries. Appropriate angry behavior means that there is warning before action."

Dogs are particularly good to observe for learning how to monitor or exhibit anger. Assuming dogs have not been abused or trained to kill, they will exhibit a predictable series of warnings. First they raise hackles, then they'll pee and scratch backwards with their hind legs and tail high in the air. Gradually, they'll move closer and closer to the object of their anger. If the catalyst does not back down, then dogs will growl. Finally, they will attack, but even then it's still more of a challenging maneuver, one without biting or seriously violent behavior. At this stage there are lots of noises, nips and slobbering, but nobody really gets hurt. Only then, if that intimidation doesn't work, will they move on to inflicting superficial wounds, but they still won't kill unless trained to do so.

Anger has such negative connotations in our society that most people are afraid to admit to feeling it, much less display it. When someone enters into therapy and is encouraged to let out his or her anger, a common fear is that emotional control will be lost, that it will be like a dam bursting and the furiously rushing waves of anger might never stop. Encouraging the emotional dam to burst is often the therapist's job.

Other people have no clue that they are suppressing anger. The day they discover the anger they have so long denied, it is often such a revelation that the discovery alone is a giant step toward healing.

The next story is one of those rare cases in which the unearthing of buried anger changed someone else's life completely. Rarely in Michael's experience does one hypnotherapy session have so much impact that it is virtually an overnight healing. But that is what happened in this instance and it was extremely gratifying to Michael.

"Before this story starts," Michael said, "I want you to envision one of the nicest people you'll ever meet. The kind of man who bends over backwards for everyone. The kind of man no one could ever imagine harboring anger or doing something that could offend anybody. That's the kind of man you're about to meet."

Tom and Tuffy

Tom is a rugged good-looking farmer living in Tennessee. He grew up on a large, successful farm, the biological son of a man and woman who raised some fifty foster children who would have been homeless but for them. All of these kids grew up working on the farm and learning basic, tried and true country values.

"This is a story I take great pleasure in sharing," Tom told me, "because it has been one of the greatest joys I've ever experienced.

"What brought me to therapy was the end of a relationship. This relationship formed the same pattern as every serious relationship of my life up to that time. I'd had three meaningful but ultimately unsuccessful relationships prior to marriage, then my marriage ended in divorce and now this last relationship had ended. I would always say I was not going to make the same mistakes again. Well, each relationship was different in the details, but always with the same result. It took me a while to realize there was a pattern, that the same thing kept happening to me. My pattern was that I gave up everything I had, not just material things, but emotionally and energy-wise. I did it with my marriage and all the other relationships I had. I held nothing back for myself."

"When I began therapy, I was completely spent. All my energy was drained and I had no idea what to do next. I don't know if it's the same for everybody, but when you are at such a level of pain that you cannot function any more, you've got to search for relief. I was lucky that the opportunity for help was presented through a friend who took me to see Michael."

Tom had several one-on-one sessions with Michael, which proved helpful. Then they decided to do breathwork, a form of hypnosis created simply by lying down and breathing in a deep, rhythmic pattern. In time, Tom regressed to his four-year-old self.

For most of his life, Tom had a vague memory of having had a special pet goat. But he couldn't recall any details and no one in his family could remember the name of the goat. Though he felt that something sad had happened concerning the goat, he could never bring the memory back, nor had he ever even thought it important to bring back the memory. That was old history, he thought, whatever it was about. When he regressed, it was this memory that flooded back.

"At this time I was four years old and I had a goat. This goat was my pal. She was with me twenty-four hours a day. We slept on the same pillow; we drank out of the same bottle; we went to the bathroom at the same time. Every step I took, this goat was with me. Didn't matter where I went or what I did, she was right there. We were real buddies.

"The goats were acquired because when I was young, I had some sort of deficiency and my right leg grew crooked. Goat's milk contained the particular mineral I needed to improve my condition. That's how the whole goat thing evolved. We had lots of goats, but I picked this special one as mine. Her mother was my milk-giver; this little female was still young, like me.

"Well, a family showed up one day shopping for a pet goat for their little boy. We probably had fifteen to twenty goats, including lots of babies. But this boy picked my goat. Daddy said, 'No, that's my son's goat.' Well, the kid sobbed and cried. So, being soft-natured, my Daddy carries me around behind the barn. Now, there was no force, mind you, none whatsoever, but he sat there telling me we had lots of other goats and this little boy really, really wanted my goat, that I could have any other goat I wanted. I remember protesting, 'But Dad, this is my goat!' Of course, he talked me out of my goat and gave it to this boy.

"Since entering into therapy with Michael and exposing and digging into what has caused all my relationship problems, I've cried often about this painful incident. The picture is so clear in my head; I see my poor little goat, sticking her head out of that car window and crying."

Tom became emotional again as he relayed this part of the story. "This is where I get a little sensitive, because it's been such a joy to realize the importance of this almost-forgotten event, and what it revealed about my life."

All of a sudden, during the breathwork, the name of Tom's goat came to him, as clear as the picture of the animal's tears at their part-ing. "My goat's name was Tuffy," he said triumphantly. "The name of the girl I had just separated from was Buffy. I don't believe in coinci-dences, and this was strange.

"There I was, under a form of hypnosis, feeling slightly out of my body, looking down on myself. My four-year-old self had material-ized over my shoulder and he was pissed off. Oh, was he mad. Snotty-nosed and crying, he was carrying a little stuffed toy animal, a special toy. And oh, he was mad. I had not taken care of my little child. I gave up what I loved most in the world so I could be loved and accepted. I had to give up my beloved goat before I could be loved!"

All of a sudden, in the middle of the session with Michael, Tom, now a sobbing four year old, screamed out, "Nobody's ever get-ting my fucking goat again!"

Michael laughed as he said, "I've never seen anybody change so much in one moment. A metamorphosis was never shown more clearly. Tom was the ultimate nice guy. He lived his life being very nice, very kind, and was a very giving soul, never realizing that he was losing him-self. He was both giving and angry at the same time. He kept trying not to give up his goat, yet always, trying to be nice about it. He always gave, and buried his anger, and he stayed angry all those years.

"Then when Tom got it, when the light bulb clicked on, he got it all the way. His is the story of all stories. This change went clear across his life. He now has the ability to make choices. Nobody takes anything from him that he's not willing to give. He has redefined his giving. When he said, 'Nobody's ever going to get my goat again,' I could see in his face that he was a changed man. Suddenly he had per-mission to fight, to be angry, to protect all that is sacred to him. Bong! Bells and lights went off and he got it! Sometimes it takes years of peel-ing the layers away. Some of us work and work and work at it, but he got it in a flash!"

Tom laughed with renewed delight. "Well, it made me really crawl inside myself and get in touch with how I feel," Tom said. "I never knew I was angry. Gee whiz, my goat! Have you ever heard a baby goat cry? She was crying pitifully…

"Throughout my life," Tom said, "I didn't realize that the goat had any significance whatsoever. I thought I had gotten over it. I had lots of other goats. That four-year-old child *seemed* happy. I *thought* I was happy. As an adult I had a memory of having had a goat that meant a lot to me and I remembered being sad when she left. But within that memory there were many details that were blocked. Mind you, within my entire family, everybody had blocked the name of that goat. Reliving that memory has done more for my life than any single thing that's ever happened to me."

Tom told his story in a group setting. More than one eye glistened with tears. One woman said sadly, "It's so hard being a parent. You think you're doing the right thing trying to teach your child to be giving and loving and yet you wreak such havoc!"

"There's nothing wrong with what Tom's father did. In fact, it is the parents' job," Michael explained. "It's part of making a child strong. But in some respects, parents are doomed to fail. No matter how hard we try our best, we unwittingly may be harming our children. Yet, somehow, parenting and the family dynamic works. It's a perfect system. It's perfect even if there is pain. To get to the place where you can see that is difficult but valuable."

One of the results of repressed anger may be "nice guy power," sometimes called passive-aggressive behavior. "This is tricky behavior with which to deal," Michael said. "It's very difficult to interact with someone who's always being nice. Nice guy power is doing things in such a way that it takes away the other person's ability to respond in an angry or negative way. People who are passive aggressive usually have no notion that they are using niceness as a weapon. But the clue is this: the giver feels like he's sacrificing; the receiver feels like he's gotten a gift with strings attached."

There is another important point in this story. In every other story in this book, an animal triggers a resolution to an emotional problem, which is often the result of interaction or the wounding of another person. But in this story, it was actually a person, Tom's lover, who shared a phonetically similar name with the goat, who triggered the need for resolution. The eventual healing that took place, in this case, was a result of a psychic wounding caused by the loss of an animal.

"We are animals, too," Michael pointed out. "So this reversal isn't really a reversal, but it's important to see that in this story it is really the human who was the angel. Buffy leaving Tom enabled him to explore himself in order to heal something from long ago in his past. He really loved her. It takes that kind of strong emotion to push us to do something so that we don't experience that level of pain again. Even when Tom got really close to the memory, it wasn't until the name jumped out at him that the connection was made, and that true healing occurred."

Sometimes, as we begin to learn new lessons of acceptable and appropriate behavior, it is hard to shake the old belief that we need something outside of ourselves to show how our boundaries can stretch. Something like an animal appearing unexpectedly in a place it normally doesn't inhabit is enough to waken our awareness. A winged creature that often has a hard time taking off into flight, just as we might sometimes experience with new and unsettling concepts, is the pelican.

Jenny and the Pelican

Jenny is a just-turned-forty single mother and artist. At the young age of fourteen, she met Chuck. They married when she was twenty-one. From the start, he was verbally abusive, but by the time she was thirty, he had become physically abusive as well. When Jenny was thirty-three, Chuck was transferred and he packed up her, their two-year-old daughter and just-born son and moved them all to Tennessee. This was the beginning of the end for Jenny.

"I had always lived within fifteen minutes of my family and I had friends I'd known for thirty-two years," she said. "My mother had just been been diagnosed with cancer and was not in very good condition, so I hated leaving her. Suddenly we were in a foreign environment. I didn't know anybody, and I had no friends." On top of that, Chuck began going out and staying away from home for extended periods of time.

"Over and over he'd leave us all alone. I had a baby and a toddler, and I couldn't go anywhere or do anything. I had no money." Meanwhile, Chuck's abuse got worse, and the children were drawn into or witness to much of it.

Jenny's depression began shortly after her son's birth, but rapidly intensified. When the baby was nine months old, Jenny was diagnosed as clinically depressed and checked into a hospital for two and a half weeks. When she came out, she remained on medication for two years. During that time, her mother and father both died, and finally, Chuck left for good.

"The divorce was one of the ugliest I've ever seen or heard of," she said. "It went on and on."

The divorce was finalized at last, but the child custody battle still rages. "Right now Chuck has supervised visitation rights," Jenny explained, "but he wants his full visitation rites reinstalled. However, the kids have been seeing a psychologist for a couple of years and they've been divulging some really negative stuff that happened on the alternate weekends they spent with him. So the psychologist wrote up a report on Chuck and I took him to court to request permanent supervised visitation."

Chuck retaliated by counter-suing Jenny, charging that she was a bad mother. "He used my stay in the hospital and anti-depressant use as reasons why I was a bad mother and couldn't take care of the kids. He's saying I'm sick."

Jenny began seeing a therapist. "The therapist defined me as a battered woman," Jenny said. "I still have a hard time seeing that, but I am beginning to realize just how angry I am. When we first came to Tennessee, things got really bad in our marriage, and I got very depressed. I realize now that I was angry with myself for not having the courage to get out of the marriage and to get my kids out of an unhappy and violent home, but I didn't know it then. Instead, I just went into a deep depression.

Jenny is beginning to realize her anger about many things. "Chuck took me away from my mother when she was dying. He hurt me and he still hurts the kids; he calls them names all the time. I really do have so much to be angry about."

However, Jenny was still having trouble believing she had the right to express her anger as opposed to turning those feelings inward. "One day I drove to my therapist's office for a session," she said. "As I passed the golf course just before his office, I suddenly saw something huge flying in the sky. I slowed and ducked down to get a better look and I realized it was a brown pelican!"

The sight of a sea bird was so unusual in inland Tennessee that even the golfers stopped swinging to look up at the huge shadow passing overhead. "I knew it was a pelican," Jenny said, "because I'd seen them in Florida. But I had never seen one in Tennessee before. I didn't really think about it being inland so far from Florida, at that time, though. What I thought first was that when I've seen them in Florida, they're always in big groups. This one was alone, though. So I looked for the rest of them, but it was just this one pelican. Then I thought, *There's a lake on the golf course, he must live along the lake. Maybe he's a pet of the golf course or something.*" She laughed at her own mental processes of the time.

Jenny and the golfers watched in amazement as the bird continued, its wings steadily beating, flying low over the golf course and beyond. It did not stop.

"When I got to my therapist's office, I told him that the weirdest thing had just happened and explained about the pelican. He said, 'Jenny, pelicans do not fly inland.' I insisted this was a pelican and he said, 'Well, he sure came a long way to give you a message! Let's find out what it is.' So we looked him up and found that pelicans are about buoyancy."

Despite their huge size, pelicans are extremely light and buoyant. The brown pelican especially will plunge from great heights down into the water to stun and capture its prey, then pop right to the surface again. The large birds do, however, have difficulty taking off again. The water (water signifies emotion in just about every culture, philosophy, or belief system) weighs them down and holds them back, but they always overcome this and manage to take off and fly.

"Well," Jenny said. "If that doesn't describe me I don't know what does! My therapist and I related it to the struggles of the past years and my depression. It was about recognizing that no matter how far I sink, I will pop back to the surface. Talking about the pelican gave me impetus, too. I wanted to be more than buoyant. I didn't want to just pop back up, I wanted to move on and not get so bogged down, to take flight, if you will.

"I realized I could relate the pelican scenario to Chuck too. Even today he has the power to push my buttons. If he so much as snickers or gives me that sideways look, a sneer that I know so well, all my self-esteem goes right out the window. Sometimes I have to go see my therapist before I can even face my former husband in court. When I think about the pelican stunning a fish, it relates to me. Chuck stuns me, too, as though I was his prey."

Today, however, Jenny uses that knowledge as fuel for her anger, rather than turning it upon herself. "I'm not depressed anymore," she said. "I'm stressed. I've been through a lot, but I'm not depressed. I'm never going back to that dark place again. Today, when I think of what he's putting the kids through, I *do* get angry and I let it out! I have a right to."

Recently, Jenny started her own business and is financially successful. She specializes in wall-size murals sold to businesses for their offices and reception areas. "I've really allowed my artistic inclinations to blossom," she said. "All those things Chuck didn't approve of! And the best part is that I have more time to spend with my kids."

Another mother, who only wanted the best for her children, learned a valuable lesson from a cat. Cats have an intuitive sense which has resulted in them being an object of fear in some cultures. This fear is a result of their seemingly uncanny ability to be silent, observant and aware. Many people have an innate dislike of cats, possibly because of this almost supernatural ability to intuit feelings.

Andrea, Kira and Jingle

Andrea is the director of an alternative healing center in Mt. Dora, Florida, called The Soul-ution Center. Andrea and her husband have a daughter, Kira, and two sons. She and her family also share living quarters with two cats named Jingle and Kringle. The litter that the two cats belonged to had been abandoned on the steps of a veterinarian's office and they were being hand-raised by the staff and fed by syringe.

Andrea's family was about to lose a beloved old cat and wanted to find another. But when Andrea arrived, the male kitten she had come to look at was very sick and they thought it would die, as one of its siblings already had. So instead, Andrea chose the tiny gray female with splotches of tabby markings, some apricot shadings, and green eyes. Because it was just before Christmas, the family named her Jingle. A couple of weeks later, they heard that the male had survived and also needed a home, so they adopted him as well. Of course, his name had to be Kringle. He's taupe with orange eyes.

"Both are very sweet, loving cats," Andrea said. "Both like to sit on your lap and be draped around you. Of the two cats, Kringle seems to have gotten all the growth hormones. He's a monster twenty pounds now and a pretty normal cat. Jingle stayed petite with tiny little feet. She is very friendly—we call it mushy. She's actually Kira's cat."

It wasn't long before the family discovered that they had a living, breathing emotional barometer in the house. They first discovered this one day when Kira, the youngest in the family was having an unusually bad day for a ten-year-old. "She was having an emotional meltdown," Andrea said. "She had a falling out with one of her siblings. There's a lot of competition between these two and she got really angry, and then switched to feelings of unworthiness. This was very unusual, and not a normal state for Kira; she's generally confident and happy. But what she was feeling was that she was not good enough and nobody loved her. She was lying on her bed crying and I came in to lie down with her and listen.

"Jingle came in, too, and climbed right between us. She rubbed against Kira's face and hands and draped herself all over the child. The cat was nearly turning inside out with her attempts to rub all over Kira. The end result was that Kira started laughing at the cat, all the while still crying. However, her energy shifted and she moved toward resolution of her emotional upset."

But it isn't just Kira that the cat responds to. It's anybody who exhibits anger. "One day, I was doing financial work, trying to pay bills for the Center, which can often be a frustrating experience," Andrea said. "I always get stressed when I sit down to pay bills or do paperwork for the Center. The Center is so awesome and we do such good work there, but the money is always tight. My nerves are on edge before I even sit down to begin the work. That day I was really frustrated and angry because of our poor financial situation, and suddenly, there was Jingle."

Many cats will spread over desks and papers when their human owners are trying to work. "Kringle, for instance, will appear often, but he sprawls all over the desk. He gets real sloe-eyed, looks everywhere but at you, starts batting at things and generally makes a mess of the desktop."

But that wasn't what Jingle did. "She jumped up on my stack of papers with her tiny little feet. She sat on the papers and looked right into my face. It was very intense; her face was reaching for me. It was as though she was like pushing at me with her face. She made strong eye contact and refused to look away. This was very different from what most cats do. I finally realized what she was doing, and I picked her up and started crying, owning up to my anger and stress. After a little emotional release, I was able to return to work without all the angries!"

The whole family now recognizes that whenever anyone is feeling angry, Jingle is there. "My daughter told me that every time she gets angry and runs to her room or slams the door, Jingle will come and paw and meow until Kira lets her in," Andrea said. "If Jingle is closed into the cat bathroom (where the cats are kept at night) she will do the same thing. She always knows, especially when Kira is upset.

"We call her our first aid cat now," Andrea laughed. "It's very difficult to stay in a bad place when something is being this insistent about feeling better and loving you so strongly."

"This is a clear statement that love conquers all," Michael said with a broad smile. "Jingle, with her unconditional, unwavering love will neither be deterred from her task nor will she do any harm. This was a good example of caring and recognition, not only by the cat, but by the mother. When someone is angry or hurting, what they need is to be loved, accepted and to be heard. They don't need to be threatened or challenged or re-directed or to have their reality altered in some way. Too many parents smack their children when they get angry. That's not it at all. Nope, it's love, love love…"

Feelings, like love or hate, aren't right or wrong. They just are. You don't have control over how you feel—you can only control how you act. Once you discover anger inside your person however, it is then necessary to learn how to express it in a healthy manner. "An inappropriate use of anger," explained Michael, "is using that energy to attack, abuse or try to change someone else."

One reason for the fear of anger in our society is that we aren't taught appropriate ways of expressing it as children. Consequently, our experience of anger can often feel inappropriate and frightening.

Steven and Guy

Steven, thin, soft-spoken and gentle, is a teacher in a community college. Like many people, he first entered therapy because of relationship problems.

"I was in a long-term relationship for about seventeen years. It was drifting apart and my partner was drinking quite a bit, not that he was violent or oppressive or anything, but he'd get drunk and then go to sleep. So we never did anything or went anywhere. I was trying to work things out for myself. I wanted to clear up as many of my own problems as I could so that I could make some clear decisions and understand why I was having problems in the relationship."

Over time, Steven became so depressed that he considered suicide. It was clearly time to find help, so he entered therapy. "In therapy, I found out I was a very angry individual and needed to release that anger somehow."

Like many of us, Steven cannot remember ever expressing anger…at least not after the first time. "As a child I never saw my parents argue. There was never any fighting, yelling or screaming. Anger was not an acceptable form of communication. If I ever started anything even remotely along the lines of a temper tantrum, I was punished and sent to my room. So over the years I suppressed my angry feelings and it left me a very unhappy person."

Steven's all-too-familiar story of not being allowed to show his true feelings left him with an inability to express anger. "If I knew it was there at all, I'd push it down or divert my attention. My belief was that

I wasn't supposed to get angry. Adults in our society control themselves. It was a shock to find out that I was inwardly an angry person." But after that astonishing discovery, and after receiving permission from his therapist to express the anger, Steven still had to learn how an adult expresses healthy anger without causing harm to himself, those around him or his environment.

Steven and his partner lived with Guy, a three-year-old white Maltese with very dark eyes. "We kept his hair trimmed short because it was very fine. When he was clean, he was fluffy. He was a very patient and loving dog," Steven said.

"One day, I was working at my desk in the study. Guy was snoozing in his usual place, under the grand piano. Something, probably a computer program, wasn't working right. I started muttering to myself, low and angry. I could feel this anger, like bubbling black oil, reaching its boiling point, and beginning to overflow. Finally, a few choice words came out and I started banging things around."

Steven threw a book against the wall, then proceeded to slam the desk drawers shut. Guy, alarmed, jumped up and ran out of the room. He ran back in, ran in a little circle then out again, his anxiety level clearly high. Again he dashed in, ran in a circle and out again. As Steven continued to vent his fury at his computer, the little dog did this several times.

"I was pretty angry," Steven said. "But I did manage to hear my partner who was in the other room, say to Guy, 'What's wrong? What do you want?' " Guy dashed another circle into Steven's room and back out again. Again the voice. "What's the matter with you? What? All right, all right. I'll come. Where are we going?"

Guy dashed into the study and back out again, clearly leading Steven's partner in. His friend finally entered the study, looking somewhat amused until he saw Steven's face. "What's the matter?" he asked. "You look like you could bite nails!"

Realizing the impact he was having on his partner and Guy, Steven began to calm down. "You had Guy pretty upset," his partner told Steven. "He came and jumped up on me with his front paws several times. Then he'd run back in here and then out to me again. I figured he either wanted something or something was wrong with you."

As they talked, Guy was panting at Steven's feet, gazing anxiously up into his face. He jumped up, forefeet against Steven's knees. The moment Steven let him up into his lap, Guy began licking his face. "I petted him and told him I'd be okay," Steven said. "And I thanked him for looking out for me." As they talked, Guy stayed in Steven's lap, licking his hands and neck. Steven's anger drained away.

"After a while I really was okay," Steven said. "Part of it was being enveloped in so much love and concern. When you feel that kind of energy coming at you, even if it's from a dog, it's hard to stay angry." In fact, Steven was very touched by his dog's concern.

"I'd never thrown a tantrum before," he explained. "It was new behavior for all of us. Nobody knew what to do about it. But then, neither did I at first."

Steven didn't change overnight. "I was still learning about anger. Often I'd be working in my office at home and I would get frustrated or angry. In the past, I would just repress it and not let it go. When my anger boiled up now, I wasn't being overly destructive, but I'd pound the desk, throw things. Another time my printer screwed up and I picked it up and threw it across the room. Unfortunately it hit my grand piano and scratched it."

"I was letting go, but the way I was letting go was not entirely healthy, because I was banging stuff around. But every time I did, Guy would come running into the room and do his little circles. He'd look up at me and jump up and down on me and want some loving."

Sometimes, Guy sensed when Steven was getting angry even before he got to the breaking point. "Guy would suddenly come in, jump on my lap and calm me down, lick my face and be all happy. I'd realize that I was about to blow and he would prevent it from going too far."

Steven found that when Guy entered the scene, his anger dissipated. It was clearly an important lesson to let love assuage anger. Steven had made a decision to no longer be passive or allow others to dictate his feelings. Now he had an angel guide to help him learn how to handle and recover from these new, unfamiliar feelings.

"I definitely consider Guy to be an angel in my life," Steven asserts. Today, Steven feels free to be honest about what he's feeling, even if it is anger. He's learned to express his anger in more positive ways. "Now I can let my anger out when I need to and feel good about it. Sometimes when driving in the car, I'll do some yelling and hollering, ranting and raving. I'll pound pillows if I'm at home." Nothing gets damaged, no one gets hurt and Steven expels his angry feelings. What might have spiraled out of restraint is now in perfect control.

"The dog exposed Steven's hidden fear," Michael said. "Even when we begin to express our anger, there is often a layer of fear left over from a lifetime of denial. When Steven didn't know exactly how enraged or how afraid he was, Guy was telling him, 'I'll be your barometer.' Whenever Steven was behaving inappropriately, the dog knew it and went for help. It's a classic movie scene of the dog trying to convey a message. I don't know how many times I've heard stories of animals that recognize danger when they walk into a room; a dog that growls, a cat whose fur stands on end, animals that run and hide for no apparent reason. They are very sensitive to the energy others put out, even when we're not."

Michael offers this advice to parents who want to know how to raise their children with the skill of appropriate anger expression. "Instead of reprimanding a child and sending him to his room when he shows his anger, a better method would be to say, 'I understand that you're angry. It's not okay to break the furniture, but here's a pillow on which you can express your angry feelings safely. Get down on the floor and let your anger out. Pummel the pillow if you want or smack it around.' A tantrum is a perfectly natural way for a child to express anger. Of course, when a child has one in a grocery store an incident occurs. The parent is embarrassed or even attacked by other people if she or he allows the child to throw a tantrum. Our society doesn't allow it. However, at home, allowing a child to express such feelings with a pillow is a good outlet.

"Now for an eighteen-year-old, a tantrum is not an appropriate expression, especially in public, but it still is a good idea to go home quickly and get your emotions out. Feel free to punch pillows or scream. However, so few parents possess these anger management skills themselves, it's hard to pass them on to the next generation.

"Those who manage anger well command respect. They have learned how to use that energy effectively and what we say about them is that they have presence. They know how to use all their feelings in the moment and at the level appropriate to that moment."

Not only anger and disappointment but the expression of many other emotions can be aided by animals. Sometimes, people have an affinity for particular animals that keep coming into or having an impact on their lives. When this happens among indigenous people, they often accept that animal as their totem. It is a natural recognition of a link between the spirit of that animal and the spirit of that particular human. Sometimes they will take on a name that reflects that animal as well.

Steven, it could be said, was carrying dog medicine since this was not his first canine angel story. In 1985, he lived with another small white dog, a Lhasa apso named Misty. Misty was a paraplegic from an automobile accident. She had no control of her hind legs, bowels or bladder and slept in a box at night near Steven's bed.

One night, Steven was sound asleep when Misty began growling very softly and finally gave off a soft 'Woof!' "Hush, Misty, go back to sleep," Steven mumbled. He was drifting back to sleep himself when she did it again, a little louder. "Misty, it's late. Quiet now!" Steven said, a little sharper. Then he heard a noise at the back door, as though someone were trying to get in. His partner's daughter was expected to arrive that night, however, so he still didn't think anything of it and tried again to sleep. Suddenly he awoke with the realization that the daughter had already arrived. Looking at his clock, he realized it was 4:00 A.M. He sat up and hollered, "Who's there? Go away or I'll shoot!"

An unknown male voice said, "Oops, sorry. Wrong house." Steven quickly dialed 911 and ran to the door where he saw someone leaping over the backyard fence.

Another time, Misty actually made it up into his bed to wake him. That time he found that a log had rolled out of his fireplace and ignited the rug. Misty was not just an angel in Steven's life, she was a hero.

It is animal angels' impact on our emotional lives, however, that is singularly important to us, though perhaps not as overtly dramatic as saving us from intruders or a blazing house fire. Tom, Jenny, Andrea and her family and Steven all learned valuable lessons from their animal angels, lessons that enabled them to lead richer, more fulfilled, less stressful and angry lives.

chapter six

─◦◦◦─

Change

Nothing endures but change.
                    —*Heraclitus*

"The two strongest fears in life," Michael said, "are the fear of change and the fear of not changing. The negative energy around change is fear. Actually, in a way, it's a hormonal response. When we interact with people, objects or places for a period of time, we absorb some of that energy and it becomes part of us. So to actively work at changing one or all of these familiar things often causes stress and disturbance. We are both the energy within us and the energy reflected by us. So change is very real; it's an altering of who we are. Most of us need some type of assistance when we are about to make changes in our lives."

The following story is of a man who has always had a spirit guide and knows how to use it during the inevitable times of change in his life. In bygone eras, this was the way everyone lived.

Thunderbird and the Eagle

Thunderbird is a handsome and athletic twenty-one-year-old Leni Lenape. Despite his youthful age, he exudes the impression of a much older, wiser man, an old soul. Perhaps there is good reason for this.

His great grandfather was a medicine man. In traditional fashion, his great grandfather took the infant Thunderbird to the first pow-wow following his birth, held him over the fire and showed the baby his spirit guide, the eagle. Thunderbird was given an eagle feather headband. So strong is this "medicine" in the beliefs of the Leni Lenape people, that Thunderbird has never experienced life without knowing that he has a guide.

"It really only happens when something overpowering hits me, if, for example, I'm going through an emotional time or feeling something spiritual," Thunderbird explained. "If something significant happens to me, the eagle is there. Either I feel the presence of an eagle or I actually see one." Either way is equally powerful. A physical body is not necessary.

"I was seventeen before I actually 'saw' the eagle," Thunderbird said. "My great grandfather died and I was pretty grief-stricken about it. My mother and I were looking through photographs that covered my whole life and every one included my great grandfather. There were pictures of he and I catching horny toads together, him taking me on my first hunting trip, doing so many things." Suddenly, while going through the pictures, Thunderbird was overwhelmed with the sense of the eagle's presence. "I just knew that it was there," he said simply. To him, this form of "seeing" is as real as visually seeing.

Thunderbird buried the eagle headband with his great grandfather. The whole experience was very powerful for him. "At that time, I was just having fun in life," he went on. "I did a lot of skateboarding and surfing with my friends and wasn't very serious about much of anything. I was just hanging out and doing things with my friends. The eagle coming to me at this time suddenly reminded me of everything my grandfather had taught me. It made me remember what I came here for. I realized I was going in the wrong direction."

Thunderbird changed the direction of his life that day. "It wasn't that I was headed in a bad direction," he said, "but I got a clear message that I was here to appreciate the things in life, not just use them. Feeling the presence of the eagle made me sit back and enjoy life and not take things for granted. It reminded me that life can be hard, but I have the tools and the training to know how to work through the difficulties."

Often the majestic bird itself does appear. Just before a recent location move, Thunderbird was going through a bad time. "I'd lost my sense of where I was going in life, lost my sense of who I was," he said. "I applied for a new job to get out of the situation I was in and was really hoping to get it. Well, I started seeing an eagle every week."

Then one day, he decided it was time to go out among the trees to pray. "When I hiked out to the woods, I was remembering all the eagles I had been seeing for several weeks. When I started praying, I was overwhelmed with an amazing sensation, goose bumps, beating heart and all, and I knew the eagle's presence was there." Shortly afterward, he got the new job.

Thunderbird realizes he is fortunate when he sees others struggling to find what he's always had, an ever-present, personal, spiritual guide. "A lot of people have to find a spirit guide for themselves," Thunderbird said. "I was fortunate that my great grandpa provided me with this totem at such a young age, so I've never had to search; it's always been there. My great grandpa showed me the way through all of my early life. Now that he is gone, the eagle keeps me on the right path."

"Most of the time now I can see the eagle whenever I feel the need," he said. "It comes easier as I grow older. I usually have to be by myself and, if I sit quietly and close my eyes, I experience the rush, the tingle in my body." There will be the eagle sitting on a branch nearby, sometimes with wings spread. It's a powerful visual and emotional experience.

"It helps me immeasurably, especially when I'm experiencing or thinking about making a change," Thunderbird explained. "Whenever I have a decision to make, the eagle will be there to help me make the right choice. It gives me a strong sense of connectedness, of feeling close to the spirit. I hope that by sharing my story, more people will understand that when they're feeling something, there may be a lot more to what they are feeling than what they think or what their heads will allow them to believe."

"A large portion of our population tries to live by skimming along the surface of life, like water striders," Michael said. "In doing so, they never fully immerse themselves. They do not feel the full impact, the full flow of life. When they begin struggling they will often go more and more into the material world and have less value for the natural and spiritual world. Thunderbird got it at a very early age, thanks to his upbringing. He remembered his grandfather's words early enough in his years so that he will have the chance to immerse himself fully in life, and that includes making all the changes and adjustments necessary."

Perhaps the only certain thing in life is change. Both raccoons and squirrels are amazingly adept at dealing with change. Both also are among the most likely to be seen by everyone, even city folk, because of that very adaptability. Through a constantly evolving ecology where habitat destruction seems to be a part of man's evolution and wilderness is disappearing, the raccoon and squirrel continue to live and play as much in the midst of human habitation as they did in the isolation of the woods. Both creatures have adapted beautifully to living among humans.

The raccoon is a magical, powerful totem. Often called thieves and rascals by those who are affected by their mischievous dexterity and adaptability, they are also explorers and game players. Their most notable feature is the mask of dark fur that surrounds their eyes.

Gina and the Raccoon

Gina is an extraordinary woman who made the decision years ago to change and live her life freely and creatively, regardless of society's views of her lifestyle. She is an artist.

Gina was not always this real, this true to herself. Making the decision to step out of the mainstream of American society did not happen all at once, but when it did, a raccoon helped her make that decision.

Gina has had raccoon medicine for a long time, so she always pays special attention to the furry little creatures. The first time a raccoon came to her was when she was a little girl.

Gina grew up in a housing development not far from Washington, D.C., a place she remembers well. "It had lots of houses, people and cars," she said. "I never felt like I fit in there. But I found a special place where I would go when I needed to feel like I belonged. It was a small patch of woods, though back then it seemed large to me. When I was hurting or lonely I would go there and hug the trees and crawl in the dirt. I'd been told it was a place where Indians were buried, and I felt close to something there."

"One day, my dog, Blackie was hit by a car and my father had to shoot him to ease his suffering. I was crying and, as a child does, wondering why God did such bad things." Gina ran to her little woods and flung herself, sobbing on the grass. As she drained her grief into the healing earth, a raccoon walked right up to her.

"I raised my face and there it was," she said. "I'd seen raccoons many times; in fact, they always seemed to be around me. But this one walked right up and stood next to me while I reached out and felt its fur."

From then on it seemed, raccoons were always in Gina's life. "When I grew up, got married and had children, there were always raccoons scratching at my door and getting into my trash cans."

Gina married, had two little girls and went through nursing school. But then her rocky marriage began falling apart. She knew she could no longer stay with her alcoholic husband, and headed for the hills of North Carolina, a place she had always loved.

"I was really going through a rough time," she remembers. "I was working at a job that was killing a little piece of me every day. Our society doesn't respect dreams that don't lead to money or fame. I was dreaming what I was told to dream by the media. You go to school, not to learn, but to get a job. You get a job to be successful and success is judged by money earned. I bought into that for a while. In my busy life, I'd forgotten to look at the sky, forgotten the magic of the stars. I'd even forgotten that I had imagination. I was dying inside.

"But I'd always loved the mountains and was drawn to them. When I moved to North Carolina I found a little cabin to live in and began looking at property to buy. One day I looked at a piece of property right on the edge of the Pisgah National Forest. I saw it a couple of times and meditated about it, but I still wasn't sure. I decided to take a walk. I walked to the base of a beautiful waterfall near this piece of land and sat down to think."

It was dusk and fog was settling in as Gina sat and pondered. It had been a bad day. Nothing was going right and she wasn't at all sure she had done the right thing by moving to North Carolina. She listened to the music of the falling water and watched the rising fog, lost in sadness and tears. Then something made her look up at a log that crossed the misty creek right where the water plunged down toward her. At first she thought she saw an apparition, a spirit.

"It was the most beautiful thing I'd ever seen," she said. "I thought it was the spirit of a raccoon. Then I realized it was real. It was a white raccoon!"

The two stared at one another and Gina knew it was there to give her a message. After staring a few moments, it walked across the log and disappeared. "I knew instantly that I was supposed to buy that piece of property," she said.

But it wasn't until the middle of the night that Gina got the real lesson of the raccoon, the lesson that changed her life forever. "I woke up with the thought in my mind," she said. "I sat straight up in bed and realized that the white raccoon didn't have a mask like other raccoons. I was being told to take off my mask! All my life I'd been hiding behind a mask, trying to be someone I thought I was supposed to be. I was always trying to please others, trying to fit in, never following my heart, never being real."

Slowly, Gina began to change her life. All of the "shoulds," "supposed tos" and "must not dos," of her rearing were carefully checked for personal authenticity and discarded if they were not her own special truth. At last, she threw herself personally and professionally into the love of nature and animals she had always felt. Never again would she run her life by somebody else's rules.

"It still goes on," she said. "It happens in layers, of course, and as I'm telling this story I'm getting very emotional thinking how it applies to my life today. New stuff still comes up. There are always more psychic layers to peel."

As Gina changed and became who she was destined to be, she learned to trust her own desires and follow her own dreams, so her intuition grew and she discovered that she also had a talent for seeing behind the masks of others. Gina has a unique ability to understand and see the real person behind their projected mask.

"People put on masks," Michael said, "whether consciously or unconsciously, because they think the mask will protect them from others. But it robs them; it doesn't allow anyone else to see their qualities so no one gets to know who they really are. As long as masks are on, people are not available to the rest of the world. The mask serves as a barrier."

Masks are not always negative. The mask is a powerful mystical symbol used by many cultures to achieve altered states of being for ceremonies and for healing. Masks can be tools for transformation. Concealing yourself behind a mask can be a very positive means of changing something you want to alter by promoting the transformation. Sometimes, the simple process of dressing differently can be a method of getting to your right brain. We can create a psychic doorway we might not have been able to step through otherwise. The lesson of the raccoon is to be aware of our own masks and know that we can use it by choice, but we should never hide our true selves behind one.

All-white animals are very special in traditional cultures. Revered as more spiritual than other animals, their white skins were highly prized and usually worn only by medicine men or a high-ranking chief or warrior in Native American cultures. The man who was lucky enough to take down a white buffalo was instantly raised in rank within the group. In traditional cultures, the interaction between the hunter and the hunted is a communion of two souls, not merely the taking of one life by another. Therefore, the killing of a white buffalo would be recognized by other hunters as a choice made by that buffalo to be killed by that particular hunter.

When Charlene was going through some soul-jarring changes and went to live in the woodshed, she arrived just after a white squirrel had been born. That white squirrel was a beam of light in the darkness of the emotional cave she had entered. Over that ten-month period, whenever Charlene was particularly down, whenever she would scream at or battle with God, the squirrel would appear. Sometimes, it came so close she could have touched its tail.

She was constantly fearful of an owl or cat snatching such easy-to-spot prey. It's one of the reasons white animals are so rare. Charlene began to feel that both she and the white squirrel were in the woods to learn lessons of survival, and for ten months they survived together.

Just when she began struggling with the idea of returning to the world, away from the safety of her "cave" in the woods, Charlene watched her white squirrel choose a mate from among many pursuing male squirrels and mate not two feet from where she sat. Within a week, she was building a nest in the walls of Charlene's little shed, even as Charlene was preparing to leave. It was time for her go back to the world of people, to build a new nest of her own.

Charlene returned several times over the next couple of months, still finding it difficult to leave what had come to be a safe haven. But she never saw the white squirrel again. Somehow, she knew that the squirrel was dead. Perhaps the squirrel's pregnancy had slowed her and she became easy prey for another animal. In any case, the woods had lost their safety. Charlene knew then that she too must cross over, and transfer to a new world, a world Charlene was better prepared for thanks to her little white guide.

Squirrels are the gatherers and preparers of the animal king-dom. They are also excellent at maintaining a healthy balance between work and play, and they are very sociable. They may show up in the lives of people who need to save or plan for the future or who are too busy working to play. Anyone who has ever watched a squirrel try to cross the road, however, also knows they are terrible at making snap deci-sions.

Barbara and the Squirrels

Barbara is a tall, good-looking brunette from Atlanta who assisted Michael in a number of Natural Awakenings workshops in the early years. At the time, she was struggling with the recent death of her daughter and the resultant shakedown of her marriage. She attended a hypnotherapy-training workshop where she met Michael. It was one of those friendships where the participants instantly recognized each other. They quickly became fast friends and together, helped bring

Michael's dream of Natural Awakenings to fruition in 1996.

At that time, Barbara was also struggling with her faith. Raised as a strong Catholic, she no longer practiced her childhood religion. She had many traumas in her life and searched for faith. When she saw and listened to the Native American beliefs another woman was studying and the natural healing Michael believed in, she knew it was time to change her path, especially after Michael suggested she start looking at the animals in her life.

"My marriage crumbled after the death of my daughter. It really only held together to get through that troubled time," Barbara explained. Her daughter had died at twenty-two, although she had survived many years longer than doctors had expected. She had been diagnosed with a hole in her heart as a baby.

"When Michael said to pay attention to the animals," Barbara said, "I became aware of squirrels everywhere. But it was truly interesting when I realized that squirrels had been around me all my life. When I was a little girl, I even made a little plastic model squirrel, one in which you glued pieces together and then you stuck the fur on. I never heard of anyone else who did that!"

Deciding that she must be on to something, Barbara began to watch the squirrels with more awareness. One morning, she walked onto her screened porch to find a squirrel splayed on the screen with all four limbs going in all four directions, mouth open as if screaming. "He was just hanging there, plastered to the screen," she laughed. "Couldn't go up, couldn't go down, couldn't find a door, just hanging."

"This happened at a time when I was desperate to make a decision about my marriage. It was obvious the marriage had been over for a long time, yet still I couldn't make up my mind about officially filing for divorce. I was still trying to believe I could resurrect the relationship. With that kind of struggle in my mind, I headed off to one of the first Natural Awakenings workshops. I drove very carefully, as I was petrified of hitting one of the squirrels darting into the street."

She arrived safely, however, and before the workshop clients arrived, Barbara and Michael were sitting on the porch of his big house overlooking a wooded area. Sure enough, there were more squirrels. "I told Michael I'd been paying attention and that squirrels were everywhere. But I just couldn't figure out what they were trying to tell me. So he pointed to one squirrel and asked, 'Okay, what's that squirrel doing?'

"I looked and the squirrel was running back and forth, back and forth on top of the fence. I said, 'Well he's running around on the fence.' Then I said, 'Oh!'

"Well, I got the message: 'Get off the fence!' Then Michael told me the squirrel is about change."

Still, a marriage is a difficult thing to end.

But one decision had been made. Barbara found a medicine woman willing to work with and teach her. The animals and the Native American beliefs had their effect.

"One day I took my tape recorder with drumming music into the woods near my office and sat against a tree. I went off on a mental journey. When the music stopped, and I became aware of my surroundings again, I heard all this chattering. I opened my eyes and here were three squirrels looking at me and chattering up a storm. Maybe they thought I was a strange looking squirrel or a very odd tree. Then I thought, *Okay, they have a message for me, what is it? I'll just watch.* Well, they started playing and running and tumbling over each other. I watched them run up the huge pines and leap from tree to tree. And I got it. I heard them telling me to play, to be free and to see how high I could go."

Finally, Barbara had the courage to make the changes she needed to make. She and her husband agreed to divorce. After he moved out, however, she found that there were still too many memories in the old house. Barbara began hunting for a new home. One day, returning from a trip into a ritzy neighborhood to look at potential homes, she found a squirrel dead in her driveway.

She was disturbed by the appearance of the dead squirrel, but recognized that it had entered her space for a reason. She buried the squirrel beneath a pink dogwood tree. "This tree was very symbolic," she said. "When my daughter died, some friends gave us a pink dogwood to plant in the yard in her memory. But it died. We replaced the tree four times because each one just didn't survive. Pink dogwoods are hard to get going, I guess."

She buried the squirrel, honoring it, the tree and her daughter as she did so. "Do you know, that tree is still living," she said in wonder. Shortly after that, Barbara was able to make the final move into a new home and a new life.

"Squirrels are still important messengers to me today," Barbara went on. "I get so busy in my work, but they remind me I'm working too hard. Oops, time to go out and play."

The physical presence of an animal, as already stated in the first story of this chapter, is not necessary in order for an impact to be felt. Tom and Tuffy, for instance, incorporated a memory. Thunderbird could sense his eagle's presence whenever he needed it. Following is another method of finding a spirit guide, be it temporary or permanent. Visualization is a highly effective technique, one that has been scientifically proven effective for healing and changing one's life.

Sandra and the Deer

Sandra seemed to have it all. She had been living a fairy-tale life, a life that, by this society's standards, was the ultimate success story. And then she divorced. "I was coming out of a marriage that gave me the best of everything," she said. "That's the kind of transition it was for me. I went from having prestige and respect, with people ushering me everywhere and taking care of me to being invisible, a single, childless woman in my forties. It was as if Laura Bush suddenly moved out of the White House and decided to be a single woman with no children."

In fact, after suffering the normal grief that accompanies the loss of a relationship, it was the realization that because of her age, she was unlikely to have children that caused her an unexpected and enormous amount of pain.

"Suddenly the sanctity of love and marriage was all up for grabs in my mind. It made me re-evaluate everything in the world," she said. She was therefore already weakened and vulnerable when the next huge change came.

"My brother's wife had a severe mental condition which, unfortunately, nobody caught," Sandra explained. "She snapped one day and killed my brother, their teenage child and herself. It was a horrific murder and suicide."

This was an overwhelming, gut-wrenching time for Sandra.

The waste of the child's life, just as Sandra was forced to face a life without children herself, was a huge part of the ordeal. "The idea that a mother could kill her own child was just a devastating thing for me. I had no way of dealing with it."

Suddenly, not only was she facing an enormous transition in her life with the end of her marriage, but the world itself no longer felt safe. "When I first moved in to this house, it was like Alcatraz. I had burglar alarms and hurricane shutters that I kept down all the time. When I came in at night it was into this security zone. To me, the whole world had lost its natural order."

Her emotions were overwhelming; guilt and anger as well as grief were involved. Desperately, she sought help to cope with the total collapse of her world.

She began going to health spas. Many of them dealt not only with healing the body, but also with healing the mind. "The emphasis was on exercising all day for your body, the outside, then in the evening you did mental exercises for your inside."

It was at a famous spa one evening that she participated in a guided meditation. "The participants were asked to create a visualization to identify fear issues that were blocking them in their personal and professional lives," she said. "The purpose of this visualization was to create a way of overcoming these fears and to proceed past them in your life."

Sandra gave herself over to the meditation. Her vision took her to the rolling lawn of another health spa she had attended. "I went for miles over these rolling hills," she said. "Then I was sitting in a chair in the sun when a fawn came up to me. It was all spots and huge dark eyes. I asked it questions like 'Who are you? What is your gift to me?' and 'How can I identify the fear issues that are blocking me in my life?' "

The fawn winked at Sandra, then began skipping like a child, bouncing and joyful. "It was like a child playing in the waves of the ocean, going in and out at the shoreline, dancing back and forth," Sandra remembered. "He was inviting me to play. He told me that he would teach me to be frisky and dance joyously. I was delighted to see the fawn playing and remembered that before these negative things had happened to me, I too had been very playful and happy. I didn't know if I could ever be that way again. I remember thinking these were qualities I'd like to get back in touch with, but I was still overwhelmed by grief. The friskiness of the fawn gave me hope that maybe I could be happy in the future."

Then the fawn added a new twist. "He said that I could also appear dignified, like he does from a distance in the forest." At that point, the fawn disappeared into the woods and when Sandra looked over to see where it had gone, there stood a tall, regal elk with a glorious rack of antlers.

The meditation was extremely moving for Sandra. Wanting to better understand it, she asked a friend about the significance of deer. The friend advised her to get the medicine cards. She did, then looked up deer and elk. "It absolutely blew me away," she said. Nearly everything she read in the Cards applied to her situation.

Medicine Cards, by Jamie Sams and David Carson, are a set of cards and a book that explains in greater detail each animal on each card and what the "medicine" of that animal is, or its traditional meaning according to ancient cultures, largely but not exclusively Native American. One picks a card in a number of different ways: a card for the day, a question, etcetera.

Sandra read about a fawn approaching a demon on its way to see the Great Spirit. The fawn was not at all afraid of the demon, and gazed at it with eyes full of love and compassion. The demon's hard heart melted. The fawn finally cleared the way for all of Great Spirit's children to reach Great Spirit without having to pass by the demon. Sandra certainly felt she had faced a demon over the previous months.

"A fawn represents gentleness, too. I had developed a hard heart since everything had happened," she said. "When violence of that nature occurs, you don't know who to trust, including family and spouse—and, of course, I no longer had a husband. So I felt very much that I'd lost touch with my gentle soul and my playful nature." The vision of the fawn and its subsequent interpretation encouraged Sandra to find, as the cards say, the "gentleness of spirit that heals all wounds." Even more, she recognized that she must be willing to learn to care about herself. "I read about being gentle with myself first, then having compassion for the rest of the world. That really struck home," she said.

According to the cards, the elk is about stamina, a quality that Sandra felt she had always had but was, at that time, needing to regain. She also read about needing communication with members of her own sex and to heal her physical body. "The book literally said that I had stretched the rubber band of my emotions so far that I might create an illness for myself, and I could feel that I was at that point. So the health spa was the perfect place for me to be right then. All these things hit home.

"Both of these animal interpretations were about evaluating my energy, being gentle with myself and taking time to heal. Love yourself and be patient. That really was what I needed to hear," Sandra said.

But for her, it was even more meaningful. "The elk really represented the transition I was going through," she said. "I was the elk in my marriage. As things got tougher in the marriage, I got more and more out of touch with the fawn part of myself. I feel I have a very playful nature and a very gentle spirit, but I had to get very tough about a lot of things while I was in my marriage.

"When I divorced, it was like changing roles. I went from this very public, very successful married woman to being divorced, on my own and having to make it alone. I still felt the need to be a very sophisticated, serious person in order to survive in my own business, but at the same time, I needed to get in touch with the playful child that I'd lost. The fawn was telling me that I could be both; I didn't need to stay that regal elk all the time."

Sandra began to write fiction. She was already a successful nonfiction writer but had done little with fiction. "A friend of mine had a little fawn decoration, the kind that would go on a cake. I asked her if I could take it to be my muse, which I did. Then right after that, I found a felt elk doll, the kind you see at Christmas. I used both of them as totems for a while. I carried the fawn around with me to remind me that there was playfulness and joy in the world. And I used the elk as the muse for my writing and business life."

She also had a "rock," which a friend had given her. "It looked just like a very heavy rock, but it was made of styrofoam. When you picked it up, you were surprised because it was so light. That was to remind me that things are not always as they seem."

She kept all three things together when not carrying them around. "I set candles around the objects and used them to meditate. I would do this before sitting down to write, which I found to be very helpful."

Sandra realized that she was healing. "I was not the person I was before my marriage; I was not the person I had been during my marriage. I was retrieving parts of me I'd lost, like my playful nature, and using them to build on what I had now become."

"I really needed something to help me come out of the turmoil of my marriage and the loss of my brother and his family," she said. "I remember the fawn because it represented the playful nature I possessed before all of this happened. It was like starting over as a little child. I thought about the elk, because it had all the confidence and presence I needed in my former life. The juxtaposition of the two—the fawn and the elk—made an impression on me for a long time."

"It's so easy to lose ourselves trying to live the life we think we're supposed to live," Sandra mused. "You have to begin to find joy in life again, even in a world that feels unsettled and unsafe."

Today, after much work, meditation and conscious use of her tiny muses, Sandra feels she is in a far different place, one which includes joy, playfulness and not so many burglar alarms. Furthermore, she now feels a deep compassion for others who have gone through what she experienced.

"This is what my own writing is about," she adds. "As a result of the tragedies of September 11th, 2001, a lot of people have gone through traumas similar to what I experienced. Experiencing violent death like that means your whole world no longer has order. The violence creates a different kind of grief and needs a different kind of healing. I hope my story may be helpful to others."

"One astounding afternoon," Michael said. "a herd of deer was browsing just across a field from me. Suddenly a pack of hounds came through, running a deer. This herd perked up their ears and watched, but didn't move. The deer with the hounds on its heels ran past. The herd knew the hounds weren't after them. They kind of pranced and danced a little, then went back to their browsing. A few minutes later, from another direction, the same thing happened. Again, they perked up, watched a minute, the babies pranced and played a little and everyone went back to browsing again.

"This happens all the time in nature. The animals know when they are the target and when they are not. If they aren't, they don't worry about what's happening in the rest of the world; they just react, they don't expand into a myriad of what-ifs like humans do.

"There is no such thing as security. Never are we secure from external forces or from the need to make changes in our lives. The only security we have," Michael said, "is the understanding of our own capacity to handle problems, deal with fears and adjust to what life has thrown at us."

The animal angels guiding Thunderbird, Gina, Barbara and Sandra were there to provide understanding and confidence in themselves, which only comes through self-knowledge, so that they could make significant changes in their lives.

chapter seven

Joy

Man, unlike the animals, has never learned
that the sole purpose of life is to enjoy it.
—*Samuel Butler*

One of the first things many people forget when they struggle with painful issues—relationships, guilt, grief over a departed loved one, a wayward child—is how to play and enjoy life. It's the first thing to go, and the last to come back.

"I'm not a historian," Michael said, "but I've read that in old European cultures, adults believed it was sinful for a child to laugh or be joyous. The church didn't believe in frivolity and idleness. 'Idle hands are the devil's work' was what they were taught. We're still taught that today. Our kids are taught fearfulness from the day they are born. No wonder our culture has forgotten how to play."

Even our first lullabies are frightening. "When the bough breaks the cradle will fall..." and the fairy tales with all their monsters and "bad" creatures. If women don't find a knight in shining armor, they're doomed. If men don't slay the dragon, they're doomed. Far before we even begin to deal with the devastating lessons of those gender roles, we hear the fear—and lose our natural joy.

In our society, one of the strongest "values" taught to children throughout life is work ethic. That alone is responsible for the inability of many of us, as we become adults, to play and retain our sense of joy. Work then becomes what it sounds like, drudgery. People who choose professions they enjoy, many artists for instance, be they writers, painters or choreographers, are often scorned for lack of seriousness. They are told to find a "real" job by family and society, and sometimes even by concerned friends. Not until these individuals have become monetarily "successful" do family and friends change their tune and show pride instead of criticism. Those who don't attain that particular version of success may never gain the respect of their families. This is a harsh lesson.

Following the hard psychological work of introspection and self-evaluation, the first sure sign of a healthy soul returning to a worn body and mind, is the desire for and the ability to play.

"The absence of playfulness is how you know you're depressed," Michael said. "Depression can either be a state of frozen fear or a state in which anger is turned inward. The word depression indicates that we are using our life energy to depress some function and that function is joyfulness, playfulness, etc. If you're not sure that this is happening to you, just notice which animals are coming to you. A free-spirited or playful creature, perhaps?"

Deer were a very important creature to Native Americans and many other cultures. They long provided most of the necessities of life with their hide, meat, bones and entrails. However, there were spiritual beliefs associated with the animals. Like the buffalo, deer have often meant life itself. In fact, in ancient European cultures, the root word of deer meant animal in general.

Those who are struggling emotionally, whether it be about relationship issues, workaholism or any of the many struggles along the road of life on earth, are often most critical of themselves. Deer can be a reminder to be gentle with ourselves.

Everyone knows the characteristics of the deer: wide-eyed

innocence and gentleness. Many are the ancient tales of deer luring people into the woods. Sometimes their purpose is simply to get humans back to the natural world we left so far behind. Often, in these stories, the purpose of luring men and women into the forests is so that the unknowing humans stumble into adventures they might not otherwise have considered.

Page and the Doe

Page is a lovely blond nurse, now in her fifties, living in central Florida. About thirteen years ago, before she ever met a therapist named Michael or heard the concept of animal angels, she had an encounter she will never forget.

"I was still married then and had been struggling and stressing for a long time about my teenage daughter's drug and alcohol addictions," she said. "I was in a really negative place. I felt as if I was in a downward spiral. I was beginning to come out of denial and see clearly that my daughter's addictions were real. She'd been in and out of several drug rehabilitation facilities and nothing seemed to help. I was at a very low point in my life trying to accept her and her lifestyle.

"A therapist friend of mine saw an ad in a local paper about a therapist couple who did wilderness workshops that took people into the forest. Those who attended were supposed to backpack into the forest, carrying everything they needed, tent, jug of water and food. That was it; that was all you could have."

Page was definitely a city girl and she had never done anything along these lines. But something about the ad intrigued her. "It would be a totally different experience. I felt I needed to do something to break my own patterns, get out of my element. My friend encouraged me and I decided that I would do it, so we both signed up. I didn't have any expectations of what this would be like. I just knew it would be different."

Page and her friend met the couple leading the trip and the other participants for the first time at a designated meeting place one Friday afternoon. They backpacked into the forest for over an hour. When they came to a clearing by a little lake, they stopped and set up their tents. Already, the adventure had begun.

"I remember being afraid of going to sleep," Page laughed. "We all had single tents and I was nervous about sleeping alone in my tent. But I was pushing myself to do this and I said nothing. We got our tents situated and then we built a bonfire. It was interesting because although it wasn't intended just for women, it ended up being eight women and the husband and wife therapists. So the male therapist pitched his tent quite a distance away from our campground, realizing that the women had probably come together to work on women's issues. He was there in more of a safety or protection kind of capacity. Otherwise, he didn't participate in the weekend at all."

It was a weekend Page would never forget. Many beautiful experiences occurred. It was her first time in the forest under such conditions. All kinds of mental and emotional doors opened. One in particular stands out.

"We started out Saturday morning after breakfast with the assignment to go solo into the forest and have a solo experience," Page began. "They wanted us to spend half the day alone. I'm thinking, *Half the day? How many hours is that?* I'm a person who likes to be alone, but out in nature? In the wilderness? I'd never done anything like that before. I remembered as a child being alone in the park or in backyards and looking up at the stars. So I definitely experienced a connection to nature, but nothing this intensive. This assignment wasn't mandatory, and it scared my friend badly enough that she wouldn't do it. She did some sunbathing instead and hung out at the lake.

"But I was determined to pull myself out of this place I was in and take as many risks as I needed in order to do so. So I started out hiking and lost track of time. I had no idea how long I'd been out there. I was searching for a place that would feel right to just sit and really connect with Mother Earth and nature. I was going to walk until I found it. It never occurred to me that I would get lost. I know that becoming lost was an issue that several other women had, but for some reason, I wasn't frightened."

For over an hour Page hiked through the forest, soaking in smells, colors, the sound of pine needles crunching underfoot. After a while, she came to a clearing that encircled a small lake. "As I was walking along the path I saw something flicker over in the distance. I looked up and there was a deer."

The deer bounded playfully along between lake and forest. Page smiled, appreciating the deer and accepting the sight of it as a gift. She continued walking around the lake and suddenly, the deer, a doe, leaped across the path directly in front of her. Page couldn't believe how close she had come. When the young doe continued showing herself, darting in and out between the lake's edge and the forest, Page had to pay attention.

"When she crossed my path the third time, the doe got even closer to me, then stopped and looked straight into my face," Page said, smiling at the memory. "We were face to face. She had this incredible, playful, joyful look and finally, I got it. She wanted me to play with her!"

Page began mimicking the movements of the deer. She darted and hopped between the trees as the deer bounded in circles around her. "I don't know how long we did this, but it lasted at least five minutes," Page said. "I will never forget it; I will never forget the look on her face. She wasn't going to leave me alone until I played with her. It felt like she was sent to me to teach me about joy, to bring fun and playfulness back into my life.

"I went back to camp and shared the story. I felt very special. The child part of me loved the feeling of being singled out by the doe. I knew she'd been sent to me. I'd been in this place of doom and gloom for such a long time because of my daughter's struggle with addiction. Now I got the message. What was important to me, no matter what happened to my daughter, was to get back in touch with the joy and playfulness in my life."

That was Page's first experience with deer medicine. Since then, she has had several close encounters with deer. "Every time a deer comes that close to me, I've gotten the same message. Okay, whoops, once again, I'm not paying attention to the joy in my life. Time to play!"

She has also taken many more forest hikes and solo walks. What began that day has become a life-long passion, an ongoing connection to nature that Page appreciates every day of her life. Her daughter still struggles with drugs, and Page still struggles with accepting her daughter's addiction. Always, though, she has a place of joy to which she can return when times get rough.

"I think the absence of happiness and joy is a learned behavior," Michael said. "Anything that makes us feel badly about life or its circumstance is learned. The presence of joy in our lives is becoming dangerously scarce. Some families have repressed it for so long that you could almost say the lack of joy is becoming genetic. Yet, the idea of playful aggression is an essential part of childhood play. It's an aggression without malice and it leads one to laugh. It teaches you how to laugh about fear and anger and communication. But today, most of us don't learn that in our childhood. People have to be taught to play today. They truly don't know how.

"Mud is great. If ever my dream comes true and I get a permanent place for the Natural Awakenings workshops, I'll be sure to have a mudhole. I will teach people how to rejoice in the earth itself, the soil that is our foundation. People are afraid of getting dirty!" Michael's dimpling face registers utter happiness. "I've seen numerous people break out and find the joy in their lives because of one good episode in a mudhole. Squirt guns are great too. They rank way up there. And if you don't like the gun concept, get a squirt frog or bottle or something."

Everyone who knows Michael has heard the story of his working with a neglected five-year-old child who had been taking care of herself for the previous year. Play was completely beyond her comprehension. As they were walking together one day, they stumbled across a mudhole. With no warning, Michael, a large man, plopped down in the middle of it. The child stared in open-mouthed astonishment. It took a little coaxing, but before long, both were covered head to toe with mud, shrieking with joy. The child's life completely turned around. Michael has also done this with adults. "Laughing is magical, healing," Michael said. And apparently, so is mud.

Animals themselves are excellent teachers. Anyone who has watched a dolphin surfing the bow wave of a boat or an otter on a mudslide, will quickly understand the concept of play. "An otter can find any little thing, a rock, or a clam, and have a blast with it," Michael said. "These creatures exemplify joy and love of life."

The beaver, a water creature, provides some of the oldest medicine in the Native American culture. The oldest known pipe, the one associated with the Lakota tradition of the White Buffalo Woman, is kept with a beaver medicine bundle. Beavers have one of the most beautiful pelts in the animal world, which, of course, led to its downfall. It also has teeth that keep growing throughout the animal's life. Thus personal hygiene can be a reminder to humans when the beaver is around.

But sometimes, the value of an animal's message lies in the fact that it is *not* doing what we expect it to do. Today, what do we think of when we think of beavers? Industriousness, the busy beaver, of course.

Jennifer and the Beaver

Jennifer and her husband Ed are always busy. They sell their artwork on the weekends in a store where tourists are plentiful, and they work on their artwork during the week. Occasionally they travel to powwows and art shows where their unique skills attract a great deal of attention. But during one period in the year 2000, they were even busier than usual. They had just come through an intense round of several deaths and illnesses in their circle of close friends, which left their work undone and their emotions frayed. They were frantically trying to rebuild their depleted stock when Ed's father died suddenly. Two weeks later, Jennifer's father passed away and her distraught mother fell and broke her hip. While her mother was in the hospital, Jennifer and Ed decided that her mother would move in with them once she came out. As before, this repeat round of responsibilities and grief kept them from doing the work that paid their bills.

"Less than a month after our fathers crossed over and just before my mom was moving in with us, Ed insisted that we really needed to just go out on the Itchetucknee River and paddle kayaks," Jennifer said. "I was so frazzled at the time that I thought I was going to lose my mind. I really thought he was crazy to take the time to go play. But when we took the boats out onto the quiet water and the otters began to play hide and seek with us, it didn't seem quite so crazy. I enjoyed them, of course, but still, I was so tense I felt like I was going to explode. The whole world seemed like an unbearable weight on my shoulders and it felt like no matter how hard I worked, I'd never get caught up, never mind get ahead of the game."

Ed needed to get out and do some energetic paddling to work off his emotions and frustration. But that wasn't what Jennifer needed. "I told Ed to go ahead and paddle if he wanted to. I just wanted to poke around some and take my time."

So Jennifer drifted downstream and tried to relax and let the water take away her tension. It was a chilly day in January and the sun was shining through the leaves onto the water. The sun's rays felt good and warming, even healing.

"I was making a real effort to live in the moment," she remembers. "After a time, as I was drifting lazily downstream, I noticed something moving near the shore. Coming closer to shore, and taking care to be quiet, I saw the biggest beaver I had ever seen. It must have weighed fifty or sixty pounds. He was up on the shore among the trees grooming himself. He was very focused on cleaning his fur and he was sitting in a sunny spot in the leaves. He didn't appear to notice me at all.

"After cleaning his fur, he began picking at his toes. It made me stop and think. The thought of a warm bubble bath came to my mind as I watched this huge beaver. How long had it been since I'd taken the time for a long, luxurious bubble bath or time to groom my feet? I couldn't remember the last time and I've always loved the luxury of pampering myself and careful grooming."

As Jennifer continued watching the animal, the beaver finally finished grooming himself. Then he began to shove leaves into a large pile in the sun. He took three turns around in the middle of the leaves much like a dog does before it lays down to sleep. He yawned a big, beaver-toothed yawn and curled up in the sun for a nap.

"The happy serene look on his face was something I had never seen before," Jennifer laughed. "I'd never seen or heard of a beaver taking a nap. Beavers are always portrayed as busy. I was amazed that this one was taking a snooze during the day and outside of the den. This new message hit home hard with me. Even beavers take time off for themselves! As I drifted downstream, away from the sleeping beaver, I realized that it was all right for me to take time out of my hectic life. I promised myself that not only would I take more time to relax, but when I got home I was going to prepare a nice, hot bubble bath and spend an hour preening!"

"People worry a lot these days," Michael said. "We fret about the past and worry about the future. We have a very hard time staying in the present. We're either afraid of something that might happen in the future, or we're sad about something that happened in the past. I think it goes way, way back, and has to do with being thrown out of the Garden of Eden, and having all that knowledge. Without knowledge, humans would be like all the other animals. I doubt there's a single duck out there worrying about whether he's a good duck or not. It just lives in the moment and is a duck."

Birds as well as creatures like deer and beaver have been assigned symbolic roles. The value assigned to hummingbirds by books, by tradition and by those who have watched them, is joy. Their minia-ture, jewel-like beauty pulls instant "ahhs," and "ohhhs" from the mouths of those who catch an unexpected glimpse of the tiny birds. Unlike dolphins or otters who show us how to play, the joy humming-birds represent is the happiness that they inspire in the hearts of those who see them. When watching them, it is easy to feel the joy of wit-nessing their unique and exquisite existence.

Michael recounted the story of a therapist from New York City who attended a weekend workshop for therapists in Sedona, Arizona. The all-glass room where the workshop was held hung over the top of a tall precipice, looking out into nothing but space and sky. At the beginning of the weekend the leader had everyone reach into a large clay pot and draw out an animal rune. Rune stones are small stones painted with pictures of animals. "One man drew a hummingbird out of the pot," Michael remembers. "He didn't like it, and thought it was-n't very manly. So he threw it back into the pot and drew another. Of course, he got the hummingbird again. He couldn't believe it."

The group went through a weekend of sometimes excruciating self-assessment work. It soon became clear to others that this man was in fact, rejecting joy in his life—just as he had rejected the humming-bird rune stone. By the end of the weekend, he had begun to recognize this himself.

"At the end of the workshop, we were all sitting in a circle talk-ing about the results of the weekend and this man began talking about the hummingbird. He said he now recognized that joy can come in many forms. He had been trying to pick and choose the form he thought it should be. Suddenly, as he talked, a hummingbird flew right up to the window opposite him and began tapping the window with its beak! He couldn't believe it." In fact, everyone had a hard time believ-ing it, since the bird had to have come hundreds of feet up a steep canyon wall to get there. It was as if the bird had appeared from nowhere. "He really got the message that he could throw back the joy that comes to him, just as he threw back the rune stone, but he could-n't deny that he did have joy in his life."

The hummingbird is a unique presence in the avian world. It is the only bird that can move its wings in a figure-8 pattern, the symbol of infinity, the link to past and future, cause and effect. Because some species migrate up to 2,500 miles, the hummingbird is also a symbol for accomplishing the impossible. Hummingbird medicine is closely con-nected to flower medicine. The magic of both is about healing and finding joy. Flowers have long been used for medicinal purposes and a bouquet of flowers has often been used to heal a wounded heart and bring happiness.

Michael and the Hummingbirds
This bird played a profound role after November of 1997, when Michael and his significant other broke up. The reverberations were felt far and wide among the many people whose lives they had touched over the years. Their stormy courtship, their incredible personal growth, courageous digging into their own dark and gritty psyches to determine and overcome their problems, as well as the impact of those problems on their relationship and on their close friends, could fill a book of its own. But after years of growth and evolution, they had finally come to the point where it was time to part.

"I was not in a good place at all," Michael said. "I not only was devastated by the breakup, but I was experiencing difficulties in my business and I sure was having problems with my self-esteem."

In the struggle to find himself, Michael had closed a lucrative office-based therapy practice in favor of working with people in their everyday environment. He felt that this offered a more natural setting to those who needed more than a formal one-hour session, who were sometimes stifled in the stilted air of an office or who couldn't afford the hefty fee necessitated by high overhead costs. He wanted his gift to be available to all who needed it, but had to figure out how to support himself at the same time. He had a longtime love of fishing, so he got his commercial license and set out on the high seas to prove and find himself and to regenerate his spirit. He plied the waters for some time, and finally, the moment came when he had to return to land and pursue the struggle of determining why he could not make the most important relationship of his life work.

"I was really low," Michael remembers. "A friend offered me the use of her cabin in the woods that had been built with the environment in mind, so I went there for a while. I was close to nature, which was always very healing for me.

"Outside the window next to my bed was a hummingbird feeder. I filled this with sugar water and immediately the hummingbirds arrived. When I lay on the bed, they were less than four feet from my head. We were separated only by the large picture window."

Every morning the hummingbirds awakened him at the crack of dawn by the loud "brrrrmmmm" droning of their wings, audible through the window. After a while, Michael realized he was watching a family of five, two adults and three offspring. He began to look forward to seeing them every day. Despite his situation, they were reawakening joy in his heart. "I knew that hummingbirds are the messengers of joy," he said. "But I hadn't been feeling much joy."

Michael was still grieving openly over the loss of his love. All of his friends suffered with and for him. But as he grieved, he also gained insight into some of the things which he had done to hinder the relationship. Slowly, healing began. "I realized that the hummingbirds were a major part of my healing," he said. "Every day, like clockwork, they came. It didn't matter how low I was or how hard I grieved, they were there, reminding me that I had joy in my life. I loved to watch them.

"Over time, as I healed and perhaps as an escape...well, no perhaps about it," he grinned ruefully, "I threw myself into my work so hard that I became too busy to do much else, including enjoying my surroundings. I forgot to enjoy the beauty around me. Work was all that mattered. Then one morning, the hummingbirds weren't there. I waited, but nothing. I was very sad that day."

The next morning they still did not return. "I really missed them," Michael said. "A year earlier I would have taken them for granted, appreciated them briefly, but never have gotten so caught up in them that I could miss them so." Another day went by. No hummingbirds, no joy. The feeder appeared to have plenty of sugar water so that wasn't the problem. Another day went by.

"Finally, after four days, I went out to the feeder and smelled the contents. The sugar water had turned to vinegar. In my ever-increasing haste and busy-ness, I had started to make the sugar water ahead of time and refrigerate it. It had gone sour. Suddenly, I realized I wasn't very joyful. I had gone sour, too."

He cleaned the feeder, made fresh sugar water and the next day, the brilliant little hummingbirds were back. Michael was delighted.

"It was a big lesson for me," he said. "I realized that if we become sour and put out vinegar in our lives, we won't get much delight in return. And I also realized that for me, too much work leads to a disagreeable, acidic attitude in my life. I was beginning to learn my own truths, what I needed to be happy.

"I thank the hummingbirds for teaching me the lessons of maintaining joy in my life," he said...sweetly.

chapter eight

Love

By heaven, I do love, and it hath
taught me to rime and be melancholy
—*Shakespeare,* Love's Labour Lost

Like many people, Charlene met Michael because she was going miserable and depressed over a botched love affair. Her soul, caught up in wanting and needing love from one particular man, had slowly starved to death under the false assumption that she received love from no one, at no time. In her hunger for one man's love, Charlene began the search to the ends of the earth, the ends of her soul to find what she was missing. Nothing else could have sent her on such a spiritual quest as the hunger, the need for love.

"The single most frequent reason people come to me in my practice and the practice of other therapists I know, is relationship problems," Michael said. "Love is the greatest motivator to grow that exists. Going through pain to the point of giving up usually comes because of a relationship failure. It won't come from being incapacitated or diseased or losing your job or failure in other areas of your life; it will be from love.

"I once heard Harville Hendricks, author of *Getting the Love You Want* say, 'Love is the only force in the universe strong enough to hold us against our discomfort long enough to decide to do something different.' It's the only definition I've ever heard that makes sense. Why else would God have made this emotion called love? Why would He have created something so wonderful that at the same time can feel so terrible?"

It is probably safe to say that everyone in the world wants love in their lives, that without it some people have been known to even give up the will to live. In the overall pattern of life, love is a goal. Love is a sign that what you are doing is right, is congruent, is on target. Life and love are synonymous to many of us. But the struggle to find it, and then keep it, can sometimes take a lifetime.

We have related many stories about dogs in the previous pages. There is a reason for this. Dogs are one of, if not the closest, to us of any other species in the animal kingdom. It can be amazing just how close, how loyal, even how sacrificial they can be. Few animals show their love so completely.

Diana and Jack

About five years ago, Diana and her husband suffered several business setbacks. The family, which included their thirteen-year-old son and a brown, shorthair, sixty-five-pound mutt named Jack, had to move from a house with a big fenced-in yard where Jack was free to run, to a condominium. Suddenly, the family was forced to walk Jack several times a day. At the time, Jack was about six years old.

The move was highly stressful for the family on an emotional level, as it would be for anyone whose business suffers. Daily, Diana and her husband discussed the business, their concerns, fears, and possible solutions. Diana, trying to hold family and home together through this frightening time, was not coping well. She previously had been searching for meaningful work of her own and was struggling with health problems on top of everything else. Her frustration with western medicine and its apparent ineffectiveness escalated during this time. The need for dog walking was just one more annoyance on top of so many seemingly far more important things.

"I complained about all of this," Diana said. "Every day I complained about what a pain in the neck it was to have a dog. What a hassle it was to have to stop everything else I was doing to walk this dog, like I didn't have enough to do already."

Slowly, over a period of about three weeks, a lump began growing on the side of Jack's neck. Soon, it was larger than a golf ball, but not quite the size of a tennis ball. Apparently it itched or bothered him in some way, because he began scratching at it until his hair had fallen out, and the growth was raw and sore looking.

"My first reaction," Diana remembered, "was, 'Oh no, one more thing to deal with.' And for a while, I just didn't try to deal with it. Then one evening I was sitting with Jack in the living room when suddenly something popped into my head. I believe to this day that I was sent a message. It was so clear and so sudden. It occurred to me that Jack had heard me complaining about him every day and he felt badly that he was causing me all this stress. So he was checking out. He thought he was responsible for my misery. I looked at him, and I knew it was true.

"I got down on the floor next to him. I took his head into my hands and looked straight into his eyes. Then I said, 'Jack, I am so sorry. I didn't mean what I said. This is all about me, it's all my stuff. I've been really stressed out, but it's not about you. Please forgive me. We love having you in our family and we want you around for many more years. You are part of our lives. I will gladly take you for a walk every day. We love you.'"

The next morning the tumor was completely gone; the hair around it was completely grown in and glossy, and there was no sign of anything ever having been there. It was a very powerful lesson to Diana.

"This happened at a time of my life when I had just begun studying and thinking about energetic and holistic approaches to healing. I was still learning and uncertain about a lot of things. This was clear, living proof to me that I was on the right path. It's really what pushed me to pursue these studies more deeply.

"I also learned the power of the energy we put out and how it affects those around us. I learned the power of words. Ever since that experience I and everyone in my family are so much more careful about what we say and the kinds of energy we put out. This was the clearest proof anyone could have wished for. I'm very careful now about what I say."

At the time, it also changed not the stress level itself, but the way in which Diana was able to cope with the stress. "It didn't make our problems go away, but it made me so much more aware of what is important," she said. "This experience gave me the confidence, not only to pursue yoga as a career, but to explore energetic healing modalities for myself and others. I am still learning and will be a lifelong student of esoteric energy."

Today, Diana is a yoga teacher. She lives in a nice, big house with her husband, their son and their dog Jack, an eleven-year-old mutt who has a large, wonderful yard to run around in once again.

"Throughout the course of my practice," Michael said, "I've seen a number of instances where people's emotional states are really expressed through their bodies. In some cases, the mind and body are so separated, the mind so caught up in intellect that it refuses to hear the body. The body then has to communicate through various manifestations.

"Even my old-fashioned, concrete way of thinking still is amazed by some of the things I've seen. Our pets and our children can manifest our stresses. In some way they are inter-psychically connected to us. This is about being mindful. In Diana's case, I don't believe that the words themselves did the healing, but that the words accurately described what her energy inside was doing. When she went from resenting the dog to loving and appreciating him, she changed the energy field. That's what caused Jack to get better."

"Acceptance is what heals. Love, forgiveness and healing all come after acceptance," said Michael.

Greg and the Cats

Greg is a therapist who, like most people, has struggled with relationships. The struggle can become so daunting that we pull back, hide our innermost selves from the very ones we love in an effort to "protect" our hearts. Little do we realize that what we are really doing is starving our hearts and making it even harder for love to find us.

When he was forty-five, Greg attended a workshop put on by a pair of Native American teachers, approximately five years before our interview. "At this workshop, which was held in a rustic lodge in Ocala, Florida, we were surrounded by sandhill cranes," Greg remembers. "There were all kinds of creepie-crawlies and animals everywhere. I remember this so well. We did a give-away around the fire and when I went up to the fire, I intended to give away my fear of creepie-crawlies. But the words that came out of my mouth were that I gave away my fear of animals. Until that moment, I didn't even know I was afraid of animals!"

About a week later, Greg was driving along a quiet road when he saw a cat that had been hit by a car lying on the side of the road. "I really thought it was dead," he said. "But for some reason, I turned around and went back, got out of the car to look at the cat and it was alive. I picked it up gently, took it to a vet and they cared for it for about two weeks. It cost about $1,500, but they saved it. I named him Lucky Leo. That was how it began and soon I started to rescue cats."

It was slow at first but anytime you start something, as Greg put it, "The Spirit seems to help you along the way." At any one time Greg and his girlfriend had, between office and homes, inside and out, twenty-five to fifty cats that they were healing and feeding.

Greg certainly was over his fear of animals—at least cats. He even purchased a couple of Persians and shorthair exotics "because I had just fallen in love with cats."

About this time, coincidentally, a longtime friend from Greg's hometown sent him a picture of Greg when he was a very young boy. The picture included Greg's brother, his grandfather and two lion cubs. "I had completely blocked this memory," Greg explained. "When I saw that picture, all of a sudden, all these memories came flooding back and it was a very emotional time for me."

When Greg was born, he had colic. His frazzled mother had no idea how to care for him. After struggling for about two weeks, she snatched up her new son, ran downstairs with him and threw him at her father, crying, "Take this kid. I don't want him!"

From that moment, Greg was really raised by his grandparents to whom, he believes, he owes his life. Greg's grandfather was a zookeeper in Pittsburgh and occasionally brought sick animals home to nurse. "When I was very young, he brought home sets of baby lions when their mothers weren't able to care for them. He would bring these animal babies home and we'd raise them until they got big enough to go back to the zoo. We bottle-fed them. If I close my eyes, I can still remember them."

Greg was silent a moment while he was relating this story, and now, several years after the memory had returned to him, he had a new realization. "Ahhhhh!" he cried. "My mother was a very anxious mother. She was like a mother lion who did not know how to take care of her cubs. Isn't it interesting that my grandfather did the same thing for the lion cubs that he did for me? I never made that connection until this moment.

"Anyway, it was always very sad because my brother and I would get attached to those lion cubs, then they'd be taken back to the zoo." Greg still did not realize the real meaning behind those early years until at last, after forty years, that fateful picture jogged the memories back.

"My brother and I left my grandparents' house when I was seven," he continued. "From seven to about forty five, I never had another pet."

Greg was not yet sure why. Meanwhile, the cats continued to come to the adult Greg.

"There was one cat that was definitely my favorite. His name was Lasher and he was a black, shorthair exotic with really big, wonderful eyes." Greg himself has big, cat-like eyes which he closed as he relived the memory.

"He would sleep across my chest or on my throat. He was very comforting to me and I imagined I was comforting to him. We came home one day and he was in the shower, all curled up and barely able to breathe. Because of their punched-in faces, shorthair exotics have all kinds of breathing problems, but this was clearly something way beyond that."

Greg rushed Lasher to the same animal hospital which had helped him start on his cat venture. "While I stood there the vet took him in the back and he died. She brought him back out to me, wrapped in a white cloth and put him in my arms. I was already crying. But then I started sobbing, little kid sobs, the kind where you can't catch your breath. I hadn't heard that come out of me in a long time. Then all of a sudden this voice came into my mind. It was angry and it was a small child's voice, saying, 'Don't ever love anything, because it will die or go away.' "

The words were a revelation to Greg; they described his own relationships with people.

Neither of Greg's parents were physically affectionate people. "My mother was unpredictable and hysterical. She could become very angry very quickly. I learned to fight as a child and was always slightly angry. I suppose that I learned to practice the philosophy 'the best defense is a good offense.'

"I remember the first time I ever touched another human being in a non-sexual way was in graduate school. We had an exercise in which we paired up with somebody we didn't know and we just kind of touched each other. It was an amazing thing. I realized that up to that point, I had been virtually untouched, un-caressed. I had married a good woman, but one who was not interested in touching or caressing. She just wasn't made for those dimensions. But that's what I was starved for. And that's what the cats do so well. They touch you, climb on you and it is such a wondrous feeling. They rub their whole bodies on you; they don't hold back anything."

Greg had been involved in several love affairs besides his broken marriage. But for the first time, he clearly saw his own contribution to the failure of these affairs. "I could never accept love. I could give it, or thought I could. But I am now beginning to be able to accept love, because the cats have taught me how."

"The truth is," Michael said, "that if Greg couldn't receive love, he probably wasn't giving it very well either. Love is pretty much a two-way street and the old saying that you get what you give is really true. I do believe that he was giving the best of himself that he could give at the time. But when he had that revelation with the cats, it was like a door opened onto a whole new vista of what love could really be."

Greg is still not sure whether a pet died when he was a child or whether the lion cubs going away was like death to a tiny boy. Whatever the incident, he feels much clearer about his own ability to love today. "I think that's why cats came into my life," he said, "to teach me that I can love. And to be okay with being loved."

Today, Greg lives with his beloved wife of three years, two dogs and two cats.

In the summer of 2002, Charlene was struggling with yet another floundering relationship. It had been six years since she left her little cave in the woods and emerged into the sun-filled light of a small cabin on a lake and the knowledge that despite unexplainable behavior and meeting the demon on the threshold, there were people in this world who loved her. She said, "My beautiful, small cabin was the result not of my financial prowess, but of the labor and love of friends who assisted me in its creation. At a time when I had nothing by earthly standards, I had started over from scratch. But I still had a lot to learn."

A couple of years later, she began a new relationship. Although it started off with a great deal of energy, it quickly became apparent that the two were nothing alike and their differences got in the way. Yet, they still felt something. They broke up a couple of times but kept coming back together. By now, Charlene had enough training and therapy with Michael and work of her own to understand relationship dynamics in a whole new way. One reason she kept coming back to something that looked impossible on the surface was a new, very strong belief that most of what bothered her in any relationship was of her own doing. "I wanted to know about these things; I wanted to heal my own issues. I wanted never again to have to leave someone I loved because I had no idea of how to make a relationship work," she said.

By the time of the next story, Charlene was again grappling with the idea of separating from this important person. This always meant torment for her. "Whether or not I initiate a breakup, one of the hardest things I have faced is my own sense of guilt, of being a bad person, even of having killed something," She said. "Such a feeling makes both breaking up and staying put very difficult, since staying because of fear means living with a sense of entrapment."

Finally, regardless of whether they stayed together or broke up, what Charlene most needed was to know what love was. After all the hard work and digging into her deepest dark places, Charlene realized that she didn't know. This is her story, but we have changed the name of her friend.

Charlene and the Swallows

It was an hour before sunset when Charlene first saw the swallow, swooping low around the boat. She noticed it because on their course from Clearwater to Appalachicola, they were exactly in the center of the Big Bend of Florida, as far from land as they could possibly be, about seventy-five miles offshore in both directions. She wondered why the sparrow was out there. They had good wind from the northeast, not from land, so no storms could have blown the tiny bird out to sea. They were motorsailing on a close reach on Charlene's friend Sam's forty-three-foot Endeavor sailboat. The seas were five to six feet, the wind fifteen to twenty knots, so the boat rocked and rolled quite a bit. It was late afternoon, winds and sea had been steady all day and all the previous night. So when the barn swallow tried to land on the wire railing, it had a hard time balancing and staying put. On top of that, the noises of a rolling boat, with flapping sails and creaking rigging must have been frightening to the bird.

Charlene said, "I cautioned Sam not to move much, for fear of spooking it more. But the swallow disappeared. Over the next hour, I wondered about the bird and hoped that it was okay. I always find it difficult to see the little land birds out at sea and to know what their fate must often be. So, as we ate dinner, preparing for our second night at sea, the swallow hovered in the back of my mind.

"Our trip had been pleasant enough up to this point. Although Sam and I are passionate about sailing and we both are good sailors, our relationship issues had often rendered even this favorite pastime a trial. So far on this trip, however, we had enjoyed ourselves. I was very grateful."

A little before sunset, the swallow was there again, this time with friends. Charlene and Sam now realized that they were migrants returning from Mexico rather than Florida birds blown out to sea. This was the end of migration season. Charlene had noticed one female right from the start for two reasons. She was clearly the most exhausted of the group and her right eyelid was solid white, so that when she closed her eyes it almost looked like a cataract. "I knew that she was the one I had seen first," Charlene said.

She landed on top of the dinghy motor and instantly, two others landed on either side of her. Charlene turned to watch them and thoroughly enjoyed their interactions. It was clear that swallows are highly social birds. They twittered and nit-picked and climbed over each other. At first she thought they might be trying to mate but it later became clear that it was simply an attempt to get closer. Everyone wanted to be inside of the "sandwich." But the first female simply held her ground, closing her eyes against the twittering ministrations of her friends. Again the boat rocked and rolled and sails snapped and flapped. She spooked off the motor, so Charlene got out of the center cockpit to tighten the backstay and keep it from slapping. That seemed to do the trick. The next time the birds landed on the motor, they stayed for perhaps twenty minutes.

At that point, Sam decided he would go below for sleep while Charlene took the first watch. Within minutes, the sun began its final descent. Just then, the three swallows suddenly flew forward to the back of the cockpit where the cockpit cushions were lined up. The first female landed. She seemed to find the coarse texture of the cockpit cushion easier to hold onto and certainly, in the centerline of the boat, she had a smoother ride. She was also more protected from the wind by the cockpit curtains. Again the others settled down around her.

"They had landed not a foot from my face where I reclined in the back corner of the cockpit," Charlene said, reminiscing. "They seemed not even to see me as they twitteringly took up their socializing again. I was delighted. What a rare opportunity to observe barn swallows! Their love for each other and need for closeness was so apparent!

"Then I became aware of other swallows circling the boat. Once in a while, one of the first ones would take off, circle, and another come in. It was as if they were alerting the others to where they were. The center female never budged. She kept trying to close her eyes while the others kept up a steady chatter and fluttering about. But finally, it seemed that they had determined this was the spot. The sinking sun apparently signified that it was time to roost. Soon, six barn swallows twittered and groomed and vied for position by climbing on top of one another, each trying for a central position. After sitting stock still for a long time, I found I could move some and still no one paid any attention. This was their spot."

It was darkening and suddenly, as if someone said, "Lights out!" they puffed up, tucked their little heads right down into their breasts and went fast to sleep, six little puffed-up swallows packed absolutely as close to one another as they could possibly get. Charlene was amazed at the suddenness of it, and also felt blessed. Not only would they get some rest, but she wouldn't need to wonder or worry about their fate. It was apparent, considering that they were still less than a foot from her face, that this was a message to Charlene.

"As I sat there, riding wind and water and watching the passage of the same stars others had watched for millennia, I thought of several of the Natural Awakenings workshops I'd been to years earlier," Charlene said. "When I'd first met Michael, I'd never done group things. I had only developed friends because of my late-in-life sailing passion and through proximity to my outgoing, friendly ex-boyfriend. I'd always found it very difficult to get close to people. My shyness and lack of friends while growing up simply had left me with no people skills. But I didn't really even know what I was missing.

"The first time Michael suggested a people sandwich, I was horrified at the very concept. This was not even a formal exercise, though it probably had been with his groups before. But this time, it was merely a suggestion of something the group might want to try before we bedded down for the night. I saw no reason to get that close if it wasn't about being sexual. During that first workshop, I left the room and slept elsewhere.

"The fact that I shook and stayed wide awake, wishing someone would drag me into that other room indicated to me for the first time that I had a problem getting close. I was learning.

"One evening several workshops later, Michael and an assistant 'sandwiched' a co-therapist who was grief-stricken with issues of her own. Although they were in a bedroom, no doors were closed and all of the rest of us could feel as well as hear her wails change to sobs, to great gulps of air and finally, to calm. The healing was palpable. Michael and his assistant had done nothing but hold and love.

"When the rest of the group retired downstairs that evening, it was as if an unspoken agreement had been made. The new members had never heard of sandwiching, but the old-timers initiated it and quickly everyone piled into a huge puppy pile. I hesitated, my body shaking, my heart aching. This time, several people who were aware that I'd never been able to do it, reached out wordlessly and pulled me down. With a huge sob of relief, I sank into their midst. They made sure I went into the middle and I was wrapped about with the most awesome experience of my life. To be wrapped in loving arms that had nothing to do with sexuality was a brand new feeling. I would, forever after, want and offer to others that same sensation.

"But had I yet learned to do it in an intimate, romantic relationship? Perhaps not."

The swallows slept peacefully, riding the motion, the wind on their chests, just behind the steering column. They didn't budge all night. At 12:30 when Sam came up for his shift, Charlene cautioned him about the fluffy little line-up right next to where he would be sitting. By then it was too dark to see them without crouching low and peering upward against the night sky. Sam tried, and gave up. He sat, yawned and stretched. In alarm, Charlene cried out, "Be careful! Do I need to stay up here and stand guard over my birds?"

He said, "I won't hurt your birds. Go on down to sleep." Reluctantly, she went below deck. Sam let her off the hook and sat watch longer than necessary. So it was at the first graying of the sky that Charlene woke up, popped out of bed and ran upstairs to see if they were still there. The birds were, barely visible only if one knew where to look. The boat was only two hours from the outside marker of the Appalachicola channel, but Sam was tired and decided to go below for those couple of hours. Before he left he complained, "I would have liked to have seen the birds!"

Charlene happily settled into the seat again. "I wasn't concerned about the birds at that point. We were close enough to land and the birds were rested enough that even if they spooked they would easily be able to make it ashore. I was very grateful for their presence and that I would not have to worry about whether these few survived their ordeal at sea. I sent out prayers of blessing and thanks for them."

Exactly as the sun peeked its uppermost limb over the horizon, the swallows started opening their eyes, looking around, tucking their heads into their breasts again, looking for all the world like two-year-olds not quite ready to get out of bed. A few minutes went by and more heads popped out again. A wing stretched here and there. It was light enough now to clearly see every detail of their brilliant blues, creams and tawny buffs, as well as their beautiful little black eyes. In the morning's light, Charlene saw that they were four females and two males. Again, she was filled with a sense of awe at their presence and their lack of fear before her, allowing Charlene to be right there among them, almost as part of the flock.

Then, as instantly as they'd settled on board the night before, first one, and then another, then a third, flew up into the sky. The other three began stretching and peeking out. Perhaps ten minutes later, the two outside birds flew. The sun was now up completely. The only bird left was the original female. She sat a while longer, but was clearly cold. After a couple of minutes, she tried to fly forward to the steering wheel, slipped on the metal spokes and went down instead to the seat. She climbed up on a life vest, tucked her head in and went back to sleep, protected from the chilly morning wind. Apparently she wasn't ready to go yet. Charlene was glad that the bird felt safe enough to stay there in the cockpit.

About a half hour later, Sam came up and Charlene told him he'd gotten his wish, that a bird had stayed so he could see close up what it looked like.

"In another half hour," Charlene said, "we began hauling down the sails to motor through the cut of St. George Island. I kept thinking the bird would smell land and at last fly away. But as we moved around the boat doing serious work, she watched us but never moved. Now my heart began to lurch tiny, painful tugs that I tried to push away.

"We sailed through the cut and into the harbor, which took another half hour or so. I could no longer push away the pain. My little swallow was not doing well. An overwhelming sense of sadness began to fill me. After all this, why now? She'd rested all night long. Why couldn't she recover?"

They decided to drop the hook, have some breakfast and freshen up before going all the way into the marina. They found a spot and Sam went forward to drop the anchor while Charlene remained at the wheel. As the two sailors maneuvered the boat, the swallow began to lose her balance, slipping sideways off the vest and onto the cushion. She was gradually losing it. She began dipping and raising her head, almost as if she were trying to see something behind her. It was a motion similar to when they had been working around her and she moved her head to try to keep track of her human companions. Only now, there was nothing there; not that Charlene could see.

Growing emotional, Charlene said, "As Sam put out the anchor, the swallow fell onto her bottom against the side of the cockpit, and her little head fell back. I started to cry. I knew she was dying. As I finished my part of the anchoring job, I knelt down and stroked her, blessing and thanking her for having spent the night with me and for her life. Sam returned just as she flipped onto her back, closed her wings about her body, and passed.

"I sobbed. I sat there a long while, just feeling the scene, trying to understand what I was supposed to get out of it. I understood that I'd been shown several things; first and most obvious was the care and concern of the other birds for her. They would not leave her alone all night, despite being on what had to have been a scary, noisy boat. Then I realized that she may have saved their lives, by forcing a landing and a rest that perhaps they would otherwise have been too frightened to take. Perhaps she led them onto the boat as a last gesture of love on her own part. I don't know. The birds have their own roles to play, but they chose to share this last night with me. It felt very big, very important. I just wasn't sure why.

"After a while, I carefully stepped down the ladder and sent her off on the waves. I watched until her body bobbed out of sight.

"I still cry when I tell this story. I've seen so many things that animals appear to do unthinkingly, while we humans torment ourselves endlessly. They certainly had no fears of closeness and 'sandwiched' on a regular basis. I was exposed to how important that is to them, literally scrambling to be the deepest inside the pack. All the while, they were twittering and grooming one another constantly, even as they jostled for position. At times that closeness probably preserved them. I've often heard of birds freezing in cold weather and always, it is the ones who find themselves on the outside of the sandwich. Their behavior, then, is also about sacrifice, knowing that some may die so that others might live. It was also about love overcoming fear, as the less tired birds consented to stop in a scary place for one of their own.

"What I understood most clearly was that this was what I believe love is supposed to be. True love is unthinking, outpouring, unquestioning, no strings attached. It is always there, and other details simply don't matter."

"I know from being around you for so long now, how terrifying the whole proposition of closeness is for you," Michael told Charlene. "The terror of getting close, for you and for many others, is the terror of losing. In dying, the swallow put the final cap to the lesson that in order for one to be able to love, one must also know when to go on, when to separate. Death is timely for the one that dies; sometimes that applies to the death of a relationship too. That swallow had no fear of her own death, yet you were greatly aggrieved by it.

"What we must be able to accept in order to devote ourselves to being loving human beings is that we must make peace with the fact that every relationship has an end. At the same time, every relationship is forever. I don't believe that real love ever dies. But the physical, body relationship has a terminus, guaranteed. Until one can accept death, one really can't love.

"It's one of those things where the back door has to be handled first, before you can even come in the front door. One has to learn to say goodbye before one can learn to say hello."

Some people are lucky enough to learn all of this within a single relationship. But for others, many relationships and many endings must occur before we get the lesson. Even within those long-term relationships, levels of intimacy end. If the couple is fortunate or skilled, they go on to the next level.

What Charlene feared most was being a murderer. "Killing" a relationship had always made her feel like a murderer. The death of the swallow pointed this out to her dramatically. Michael and Charlene both feel that her fear belongs to something long ago. They don't know what, but just recognizing that has brought her some peace. Since then, she has felt much calmer about relationships. "I do not have to decide whether or not to 'kill' a relationship in order to avoid the pain of a future natural death," she said. "Today, I am more capable of living one day at a time without the agony of that decision weighing me down."

"It is the fear of things getting so good that one cannot stand it ever ending that stops most people from making the choice to love," Michael said.

In the following story, both the man and woman sense that the other is their perfect match, however, a certain level of indecision mars their ultimate commitment to each other. It took one of the larger animals in our world, rather than a tiny sparrow, to move things along. Bears are one of the most powerful, and most ancient of animal medicines. Some of a bear's mystery has to do with how closely associated it is with man. Like man, it is both carnivore and herbivore; like man it can stand up and walk on two feet. A bear vanishing into a cave for hibernation represents our own inner musings, our own subconscious. And whatever else it is, a bear is big. It's a hard message to miss.

Marc, Michelle and the Bear

Marc and Michelle are the type of people writers love to write about. They are both tall, dark and slender with the kind of good looks that make heads turn whenever either of them enters a room. Together, they are the epitome of a beautiful couple. It is difficult to believe they ever had problems while courting. Wishful single people who see them today, and even some couples, need only watch this couple to realize that truly loving and sharing your life with another human being can be possible. Their love is clearly visible to all who come within their glowing orb.

Six children, ages six through eighteen, share their union. When they came together, it was like a real-life Brady bunch, Marc with his three kids, Michelle with her three. Today, Michelle, a singer, has gone back to school to become a therapist. Marc works in construction, though writing is a serious love which will doubtless come to the forefront one day. For this story, I will share Marc's last name because it is a part of the story. His true name is Marc Boone.

Marc and Michelle are from the same area of Michigan, but they did not meet there. They met in Florida during a social event, while both were married to other people. "I immediately noticed him," Michelle readily admits. "Who doesn't? Look how handsome he is!" Marc's initial response to Michelle was the same.

Both of their marriages had been on the rocks long before their first meeting. Marc was the first to separate from his wife. But that was just the beginning of more troubles. He began drinking to ease the pain of a life gone awry.

"A mutual friend asked me to go check up on him," Michelle said. "She knew he was drinking too much and was worried about him."

Michelle did go check on Marc and that was the beginning of their friendship. "I was still struggling with my husband," Michelle said. "But nothing was working very well." Before long, she too had separated from her mate and at last she and Marc began dating.

"That first year, though, I wasn't so sure we were going to make it," Michelle said. "He was still drinking; we were both going through child custody hearings and divorces and things were a mess." They realized they both cared a great deal for each other, but by the end of the year, Michelle broke off the affair. "I was more concerned about my kids and his drinking," she explained. "I had never allowed them to be exposed to it, but keeping him away from them was hard. Finally I told him I couldn't keep seeing him under those circumstances."

It was a devastating blow for Marc. "I knew she was the one for me," he said. "But I didn't know how to pull myself together."

He began therapy with Michael while Michelle, also feeling strongly about Marc, nevertheless decided to move on with her life. She began dating someone else. "It just wasn't the same, though," she said.

They were apart a year, a grueling one in which both dated other people while Marc continued to dig deeply through the morass of his own psyche and touched into his darkest places. "It was not a pretty sight," he says with a grin. But at last, he began to understand some of the demons that had driven him. He ultimately began to feel pretty good about himself and finally stopped drinking.

"I had just had a date with this other person," Michelle said. "I was driving home from it and I thought, *This is not right. He just isn't the right person for me.* I was feeling so discouraged and sad. And right then, while I was driving I started thinking about what kind of man I would want if I could have anyone. So I compiled my list. I thought of everything I could and then I sent it out to the universe with a prayer and just turned it loose. I gave it to God."

That evening, Marc called. "As soon as he telephoned, I knew he was the man I'd been waiting for."

Still all did not go smoothly. Both had to learn to trust again, how to relate on a new and deeper level. Michelle began attending workshops with Michael, digging deeper into her inner self. "We both wanted this to work, and we both knew it would take time and energy to make it work. We had to do this differently from any way we'd related to anyone before."

And work at it they did. Of their many friends who watched and cheered and at times, disbelieved, all became thoroughly admiring of these two very courageous people. Marc and Michelle were willing to look inside themselves before blaming the other for their troubles. They were people who were so open that everyone around them bore witness to their struggles. After another year, they began to feel comfortable enough to finally bring up the topic of marriage.

But this time had to be different from their past relationships. "Michelle and I had been talking about getting married for several months," Marc said. "We knew we were getting close, but we both knew we wanted to do it differently from the way we had in our first marriages."

In neither marriage had the man asked the woman to marry him. Michelle had pursued her first husband until he finally agreed to marry her. "The whole marriage felt out of whack after that," Michelle explained. "I felt I led the marriage and it really wasn't good. I didn't want that kind of dynamic again. I wanted the man to be the one to ask this time."

Marc and his first wife had just fallen into marriage, assuming that was the way they were heading without a real request being made by anyone. "I always felt I'd missed out on some traditions I would have liked," Marc explained. "I wanted to be the instigator, for one thing. I didn't want to just be eating dinner at the table one night and say, 'Oh, by the way, honey, will you marry me?' So I wanted it to be the right time. What is the right time? I didn't know, but I knew somehow something would happen and I'd know."

So Marc began to look for his sign. He was not going to rush this one. It was too important. He wanted to start their marriage off on a good footing. He wanted a sign that he was right about the timing, right about the marriage. "I didn't know what to ask for, but I figured it would be big. I wanted there to be no doubt that it was the right time. I didn't know what it would be, but I knew I'd know it when I saw it," he said. "I'd been through enough by then, had learned enough, that I had faith that when the time was right, my sign would appear."

That summer Marc and Michelle went to northern Lake Huron in Canada to vacation with Marc's family on his father's thirty-six-foot trawler. "It was a place where we traveled every year when I was a kid," Marc explained. For thirty years Marc, his two sisters and three friends would spend three weeks on the lake with Marc's parents. "We'd cruise the islands and coves, fish and water ski. We all loved it and by this time, we knew the area very well."

This would be Michelle's first time at this special family vacation area and everyone was excited about sharing it with her. Marc's family knew about one hundred different anchorages from their travels over the years. One evening, they pulled in to one of their favorite anchorages, a place they called Oak Bay. As they pulled up to the landing they were greeted by three dogs, two of indiscriminate mottled colors and one pitch black. They were domestic but skittish and hung around the boat as though looking for handouts. When none were forthcoming, they took off, apparently in search of better offerings.

The next day, Michelle and Marc decided to take the dinghy and tour some of the nearby islands and inlets. Marc's dark eyes sparkled as he continued with the story. "We were motoring through a constricted area, between two islands with about thirty yards between the shores when Michelle suddenly said 'Look! There's a bear!'

"I didn't believe her. I figured it was the black dog we'd seen earlier so I said, 'Yeah, right!' But Michelle said, 'No really, it's a bear.' "

Marc turned and looked up. Through a dense undergrowth of trees, a shelf of rock jutted out, approximately twenty feet wide by ten feet deep. On it a full-grown black bear stood looking straight at them. Marc stopped the engine and stared, dumbfounded.

"Remember," he said, "I'd been going there for thirty years and I'd seen neither hide nor hair of a black bear until that moment. We knew there were probably bears up there, but we'd never seen one and no one we knew had either!" He looked at Michelle to see her staring up at the bear, open-mouthed. The bear stared solemnly, pointedly, at both of them for a long moment, then finally, turned and ambled back into the brush.

Marc started the boat's motor back up and began thinking about some of the information he'd learned concerning Native American beliefs about the bear. "It was about death and rebirth because of the bear's hibernation, and healing. Also, the sheer power of the bear totem was awesome. Finally, I realized if that's not a sign, what do I need, the sky to fall? I knew my sign would have to be something out of the ordinary and I had wanted something that would have a big impact on me; I just didn't know it would be that big!"

Marc shut the engine off once more. He got down on the floor of the dinghy on one knee. Michelle turned around to look at him. "What's up?" she asked, puzzled.

Marc took her hand and asked her to marry him.

"I cried," Michelle said. "It really was the perfect moment."

"I watched Michelle and Marc struggle and deal with their fears," Michael said. "What I felt when I heard their story was the robust, vital sense of life we all have and how the bear symbolizes this power. It deals with threats and walks through the forest calmly. What Marc was looking for most was a validation of strength. Michelle wanted a strong man.

"I don't think there was anyone who was witness to the final stages of their relationship and witness to their marriage who was not impacted, even awed by it. They'd both been open and willing to talk about every period of their relationship, so everyone knew all of their problems and struggles as well as their successes. They were an open book to their friends."

Marc and Michelle are rare people who unlocked their lives, came out of the woods and "bared" themselves to their friends. Few couples are as candid.

"Nevertheless, more and more people are willing to work on their problems," Michael continued. "When I first started as a therapist probably one in ten women was able to drag her husband into therapy under some threat or duress. Women seem to undertake the task of bringing men spirituality. Perhaps the process is linked: A woman's desire to change a man versus man's fear of change. However, more and more in recent years, even single men have been coming in, realizing the answer to relationship problems is preparation for understanding themselves. The concept of healing through therapy is more accepted today.

"It is no accident that this was a bear, or that it had such impact," Michael continued, delighted with this story and with the relationship between two dear friends.

The bear was a perfect totem for their marriage. Both felt they had been asleep previously in their lives and both had done a lot of work to become fully conscious. "We're definitely more awake now than we ever had been before," they readily admitted.

Marc's great, great, great granduncle was Daniel Boone. "I recently ran into an uncle I hadn't seen since I was a kid," Marc said. "He was married to my father's sister and knew my grandfather as a young man. He told me about all these characteristics I find in myself. He described my grandfather as 'kind of a crazy dreamer, always going off into some far-flung adventure.' The more I've learned about myself, the more connected I feel to my own heritage."

According to popular history, the famous outdoorsman actually left a sign on a tree, reading 'Dan'l Boone killed a bar,' a sign meant for the whole world to see. Marc loves Michelle, and married her, so the whole world would know.

chapter nine

Faith

The mountains, I become part of it
The herbs, the fir tree, I become part of it
The morning mists, the clouds, the gathering waters,
I become part of it.
The wilderness, the dew drops, the pollen,
I become part of it.
— *Navajo Chant*

After the pendulum of life has swung from fear and depression to giddy joy and playfulness, it begins to seek the evening level of acceptance, serenity and faith. Actually, this chapter may well have been labeled Acceptance, for it is that which brings about all evolution and growth.

"Our psychological growth work is always about recognizing and then accepting," Michael said. "For instance, once we accept anger, we have determination. Once we accept the value of a person in our lives, we have love. Once we accept our dark sides we can truly appreciate our light sides. But acceptance is the first step to all of this."

Once we accept, then we have grace. That is the peace that comes from our own acceptance and that's why we called this chapter Faith, which is the result of grace.

"The value of recognizing signs and messages from animals is that it is far easier to recognize certain traits in an animal first, and then transfer that acceptance to us humans," Michael said.

During the first Natural Awakenings workshop in a new format, every participant, including Michael, was treated to a strong validation that they were on a good path. "Naturally, when you start something new, something you've never even heard of anyone else doing, you're anxious," he said. "You're nervous, a little fearful of something going wrong, backfiring."

The last night of the workshop, one of the participants offered to do a Native American pipe ceremony for the group. "This man's pipe was the duck pipe," Michael said. "So we all gathered in a circle around a campfire down by our pond."

The ceremony began. The leader of the pipe ceremony performed the ancient, preparatory steps one by one. Just as he was about to pass the pipe, suddenly he felt something bump his back. He turned and looked down. A duck waddled around him and sat down next to him. Nobody could believe it. "We'd been talking about this kind of thing all weekend, but nobody really expected to receive validation this strongly!" Michael laughed.

As the pipe passed, the duck remained in place. Once the ceremony was finished, the duck got up and waddled back to its pond. "Talk about a renewal of faith!" Michael said. "Nobody in that circle doubted that God, in whatever form the individual believed, was there that night!" Thus Michael received full validation that what he was doing was good.

Faith represents many different things: hope, acceptance and belief. Getting to or maintaining this point seems to be the purpose of our lives. Most of us are fighters. We have struggled all our lives to survive, to understand, to figure things out in our heads. Often, the time of greatest faith occurs when, at last, we give up. Once we give up, we often find ourselves open to truth. Only then do we finally hear, see, or understand the message. It comes, then, through the heart, not the head.

Jane and the Frog

Jane is a lovely young woman, tall, slender and blond, seemingly with everything to live for. Yet she has nearly died several times. She traces her problems back to her grandfather's death. "He was my best friend in the whole world," she said. "He would birdwatch early in the morning at 4:00 A.M., looking out over his garden, and I would sometimes join him. I just loved him to death. He died when I was thirteen, and that's when I started doing drugs. By fourteen, I was really screwed up."

Jane was on a dangerous path. By the time she was an adult, she knew what the insides of jails and crackhouses looked like. Three years before, things had gotten desperate. "I was into a lot of dangerous things," she said. "Between buying drugs and guns and crazy stuff like that, I had really gotten myself in deep." And in the process, she nearly killed herself. After barely surviving a particularly bad drug experience, she fled a crackhouse and a boyfriend who had influenced her too heavily. She moved to central Florida to live with her father.

"Physically, I was nearly dead," she said. "Mentally and emotionally, I was completely spent." She was twenty-seven years old and felt her life was over.

Jane was introduced to Michael, and began trying to figure out why she engaged in such self-destructive behavior. "I wanted to learn about myself. I had a lot of time to myself because I didn't know people in central Florida, and I didn't feel like I had any friends."

Jane was a smoker, so she spent a lot of time on her mother's second floor balcony. "There were a lot of trees around that area and the land sloped down to a little swampy area that attracted lots of birds and animals. It was a very peaceful, quiet area away from the main road."

When Jane first arrived, she was vaguely aware of seeing a frog on the side of the house. Though she saw him come out of his hiding spot in the slats between the porch light and the door of the house she didn't pay much attention. She was caught up thinking of serious, life-threatening problems.

"He was a big, brownish-green frog. Not one of the slimy ones," she explained, "but rough-skinned with big eyes. Sometimes he just stared at me."

One day, Jane was sitting on the porch with her father and several neighbors of her mother's friends when suddenly she felt something land in her long, blonde hair. She shrieked and leaped up. "It's a frog!" someone said and extracted it from her hair. That was the first time the frog touched her. From then on, the frog leaped at Jane almost every time she walked out of the house.

"No one could believe it," Jane laughed. "My father and his girlfriend knew the frog lived there. They'd seen him come out to eat bugs by the light. But it had never jumped on anyone before. He didn't do it to anyone else, just me. I think it was to get me to notice him, because I hadn't paid any attention before. I probably wouldn't have paid much attention otherwise."

After a while, the frog seemed to realize that Jane had accepted its presence, because it calmed down. Instead of jumping on her, it would come out of its hiding hole, hop down the wall and over to where Jane was and climb onto her shoulder.

"It was like I had a pet," Jane said. "I had this little friend that would come visit me, sit with me and hang out with me."

Up to this point, the frog was simply a kindly presence and a novelty, something Jane appreciated but still didn't think about very much. "Then one day, Michael told me I should look up the frog in one of the books," Jane said. "I couldn't believe what I read. I was shocked."

The book told her that frog medicine was about coming back from a near-death experience. "I couldn't believe it," she repeated. "I had recently almost died and I still felt like I was slowly dying inside."

Simply finding out what the frog signified was a very powerful healing experience for Jane. "I suddenly had hope for the first time," she said. "I felt like maybe I could go forward. Maybe I would survive. Maybe I could get away from all my destructive tendencies." Jane felt a love and support from the universe that she had never before felt, one that she still has difficulty putting into words.

"I was at my father's home for three months and that frog came to me probably 98 percent of the time that I walked outside, which, of course, was several times a day. It really was amazing," she said.

Within three days of Jane leaving her mother's house for her own apartment, restored in body and spirit, her father found the frog dead. "I've tried not to think about that part," Jane said. "In fact I'd forgotten it until just now. It really was my frog, wasn't it?"

"This young woman was in a lot of pain," Michael said. "She wasn't attached to anything, didn't believe in much. She was adrift.

Drugs and music, staying entertained was all that she knew. When we started talking about the concept of animal angels and animals as message totems, she saw others responding to the idea, but she still wasn't a part of it. She didn't really understand until the frog started leaping on her. She believes now."

As we have discussed, animals sometimes live hard lives for others to learn lessons. The same is true of people. Some of us choose harder assignments than others.

The frog gave Jane hope. Hope is a problematic word. It assumes that you don't have something in your life, something you think you need. We have chosen to put hope with faith because most of us are still learning that we already have everything we need. We only need to open up or recognize it. The frog gave Jane hope, yes, but it also gave her faith in something outside herself, something greater than her that cared about her.

Pauline and the Grackles

Pauline is teacher Florida. At the time this event occurred, however, she had given up everything in her own life to be the primary caregiver for her mother, who was dying of cancer. For two years, her mother was Pauline's whole life, and it was an exhausting life. "At first I was resentful," she admitted. "I gave up my career, my desires and my plans when I decided to take care of her. I no longer had a life of my own." After talking with a spiritual friend who spoke to her of the concept of "have to/got to versus love to/choose to" Pauline chose to make her decision a gift rather than a duty and turned her care for her sick mother into a beautiful, loving experience. At the same time, she also volunteered and gave a great deal of her time to inner city kids. In the end, she completely burned herself out.

"After my mother died, it took me a year just to recover my strength," she said. "I floundered around without direction. I didn't know what I wanted to do." Pauline put her mother's ashes into a beautiful ornamental teapot and talked to her every evening when she came home. Confused, depressed, still grieving and unable to free her mother's spirit, she turned to Michael for help.

"I was dealing with several issues," Pauline said. "Certainly, the death of my mother was a big one. I had a hard time accepting it, because it had become the whole of my existence for two years. I'd given up everything to take care of her and I didn't know who I was. I was also dealing with my femininity and religious issues."

Since her divorce six years earlier, Pauline had not felt like a woman. "I never had children and now I didn't have a man. I didn't know much about my own femininity."

Women are supposed to be the givers in our society, the nurturers. But how much is enough? Pauline had given until she collapsed. She herself was empty.

She had also had a bad religious experience in Asia. She had gone there as a Christian missionary years earlier, loving God, wanting to do God's work where people needed help. "I didn't fit my co-workers' ideas of what a Christian was," Pauline said. "I left earlier than planned, very shaken and disillusioned. I realized all I knew was Christian law; I knew nothing of Christian grace. When I returned home, I sat down and asked God to teach me his truths."

At that point, Pauline embarked on a study of Chinese medicine, Eastern philosophy and Native American traditions. By the time she came to Michael, Pauline knew only that whatever her answers were, the were not necessarily other people's truths.

Because she drove from a considerable distance, Michael sometimes met her at a cabin he owned on a lake, which meant less of a drive for Pauline. This cabin was part of an one-time fishing camp that sat with other cabins under the shade of ancient live oak trees surrounding a lovely park area. The first time Pauline arrived, she went straight into the cabin for her session. Afterwards, she and Michael walked down to the lake and sat on the dock, talking.

"It was like déjà vu," Pauline said. "I was sitting there on the dock just knowing I'd seen this place before. Then I remembered. We had had a family vacation there when I was eleven years old and it was still used as a fishing camp. Being there brought back all these wonderful memories. Both my mother and I had been happy during that vacation, so when I finally reached the point at which I was ready to release my mother, I knew that was where I wanted to do it."

The day arrived when she had committed to Michael that she would release her mother. She sat in his cabin and they talked for a while. Finally, Pauline was ready and they walked down to the lake.

"It was completely fogged in," Pauline said. "I couldn't believe it. I'd never seen it like that before. Neither had Michael. It had always been beautiful and bright with sunlight diamonds sparkling in the water, so warm and nurturing. Now, you couldn't even see the lake!"

They walked out to the end of the dock, sat down and began talking about what Pauline was about to do. Pauline was a little put off by the fog. Then Michael said, "Look Pauline, there's no horizon."

"I realized then that it was a heaven and earth interface," Pauline said. "You couldn't tell where earth stopped and heaven began."

Suddenly, a flock of grackles, flew in, landing on every post and piling. "They were everywhere," Michael said, "and they were all female grackles, not a male among them."

At that point, Pauline was ready. She began to pray aloud.

Michael remembers this as clearly as Pauline does. "When she started to pray, every one of those chattering grackles fell silent, and grackles are never silent! But they all sat there, watching her, sober and silent, not moving. It was like we were surrounded by nuns!"

Pauline continued to pray and reached into the ornamental teapot for a handful of ashes. She tossed them into the lake. A little of the fog lifted. She continued praying, tossing handfuls. With each handful tossed, the fog lifted a little more.

"At one point, a bird flew up in front of me and I said, 'Mother, you've got your wings now.' Right then, I saw a golden disk in the water and realized it was the sun peeking through the fog. I continued throwing my mother's ashes in the lake and the fog kept rising. By the time I got to the last handful, the day was completely clear and sunny."

Pauline felt a tremendous release as she finished. In sudden exuberance, she tossed the teapot high into the air as well. "As it sank into the lake, I put behind me the last of that bad experience in Asia," she said. "I was ready to move on. Then Michael said, 'Look Pauline, you can see the horizon!' And I thought, *Exactly! New horizons!*"

As she turned back, the grackles took up their normal, noisy "grackling," hopping about and some flew away. "It was as though I had an audience," she said. "They were there to support me and when it was all over, they were ready to leave too."

The experience enabled Pauline to move forward in her life. "Finally, I was able to make some decisions and I moved to a new town and brought a new outlook with me. I've developed a wonderful life here," she said. "I feel like God showed me the interface between heaven and earth, and they are only a hair apart. I know my mother will always be with me. I wasn't giving her up, I was giving up all the old hurts and my insistence on hanging on to a past life and always doing for others and never for myself. And I felt so supported in what I was doing with all those birds surrounding me."

The universe continued to support her with the seemingly sudden appearance of a wonderful job and a new home in the woods. She has become a Reiki master, studies attunement and has begun painting and working in drama.

"What this story is about is the validation of spirituality," Michael said. "Pauline's willingness to move forward was supported. Also, her story is confirmation that the whole universe is aware of the passing of one spirit. When someone comes or goes, it's not in a vacuum. The whole world knows."

Perhaps no other animal inspires as much reverence among people as the eagle. Our national bird has long been the subject of the myth and history of every culture that shares its living spaces with eagle. The bird's ability to soar to great heights, its prowess as a hunter and its fierce appearance have all added to the mysticism surrounding this huge creature. The eagle has been associated with nearly every religion.

Kathy and the Eagle
Kathy is a hard-working, outgoing woman who recently struggled emotionally with turning fifty and is now entering her middle years with beauty and grace. Achieving a state of grace is something she has worked at for a long time. She's always had a strong love for God, but learning how that love fits into her life has not been so simple.

Kathy grew up in Maryland, and was raised in the Catholic Church. At a young age, her mother left an alcoholic husband and struggled to raise three small children alone in an era when divorce was still rare, especially among Catholics. She soon remarried, at which time Kathy's name was no longer the same as her mother's. At the Catholic school she attended, this fact was questioned by her second-grade teacher, a nun. Kathy explained that her mother was divorced. The nun proceeded to tell the class that Kathy's mother was going to hell. Though mortified, Kathy didn't believe this in her heart. She loved God, and had already experienced His presence many times and felt certain that He didn't care whether her mother was divorced or not.

Yet the memory of what that nun said haunted her for years to come. Kathy continued growing in good Catholic tradition, reading only what the nuns allowed, learning only what they taught, accepting that the only way into heaven was by being a good and dutiful child. "I'm sorry to say I was in my thirties before I ever questioned anything," she said.

By then however, she was married and raising babies, still within the strictures of the church. It was not long after her marriage that she knew she had problems on her hands. Her husband was alcoholic and, within a year of their marriage, he had the first of many affairs. Kathy's strict Catholic upbringing and the embarrassing memory of her mother's divorce kept her in that marriage for twenty-two years. But through those years, she finally began to question, to wonder and at last, to get angry with God.

In the coming years there would be several separations from her husband and several physical moves. At one point, she and her family moved to North Carolina. In the mountains Kathy found the solace and beauty she craved. Always aware of nature, the mountains touched something within her that nothing else had. She found a new peace and connection to God she had not yet known. A wonderful pastor who taught scripture from a more liberal pulpit, who was perhaps influenced by the mountains in which he lived, helped her through tough times. When her husband moved the family back to Maryland, Kathy had already made the decision that she wanted to raise her children in the mountains. Thus, when she next fled his abuses, this time obtaining a divorce, she went back to North Carolina.

"This was a very scary time for me," Kathy said. "I had no idea whether or not I could get an annulment. The Catholic Church was so important to me. In fact, it kept me from getting divorced for a long time. I couldn't stand the thought of never taking the sacrament again."

She was raising four children on her own and she was very unhappy feeling that she was outside the church. Lonely, broke and exhausted, Kathy remarried her husband on their seventeenth wedding anniversary.

Over the next five years, during which they moved to Florida, there were some good times, but eventually she again had to end her marriage because of her husband's behavior. This time, she began her search for answers. It began with a therapist who would later become a friend, Dr. Elisabeth Pringle, with whom Michael shared a therapeutic practice.

"By 1991, I'd been in therapy for about four years," Kathy said. "I was an undergraduate student at St. Leo's College, doing therapy with Liz and Mike and I had just married my second husband about a year earlier. We had both been going through the very involved process of getting annulments of our previous marriages. About this time, the annulments had just come through, so I was feeling much happier that I was legally (within the church) remarried. However, by then, I was really starting to question my religious beliefs."

She also had been taking religion courses at college and came to the conclusion that some of the things the church taught were immoral. "I was beginning to look at their treatment of women and other issues and suddenly, I could no longer accept all of the church's teachings. It was very painful for me." Instead of blindly accepting everything she was taught, Kathy was beginning to expand her awareness and trying to figure out for herself how God works.

She had also been doing some serious soul searching in her therapy sessions. "I was working, at that point, on being judgmental, because I had just discovered that it was an unfortunate character trait I possessed. I was beginning to realize that nobody has the answers for somebody else. I don't have the right to say that what someone is doing is right or wrong, or that something has to be done a certain way." Kathy was beginning to realize that much of that sort of thinking in her personal life had come from the church's teachings in her religious life. It was all connected.

Kathy had a sister in North Carolina who had begun to delve into Native American teachings. This was going much too far for Kathy, however. When her sister invited Kathy to join her for a weekend gathering, she accepted, but not because she thought it would be good for her.

"I was going to save my sister," Kathy laughed. "I was just sure she was into witchcraft or something with all those rocks and plant things she was doing. So I went there for her.

"I'd always been a person who appreciated nature, though I grew up a city girl," she said. "But if there were woods anywhere, I was in them. I'd had pets all my life. My children always had animals and we took in strays. I always saw the dogs and canaries and hamsters as animals, though, apart from us. I never fully understood or appreciated their places in the universe."

Kathy undertook a test of courage she hadn't expected. When she was invited to participate in a sweat lodge, she was scared to death about its spiritual safety. But she still was determined to help her sister. So she wrapped a miraculous medal in a bandanna and put it around her head hoping to protect herself from going to hell.

"I had an incredible experience in the sweat lodge," she said. "But even afterward I was scared to death I'd done something wrong."

The weekend was a real door opener for Kathy. She enjoyed the drumming, but when they began to talk about watching the animals, and learning their messages, it simply didn't compute. "It didn't make sense to me," she said. "How could an animal deliver messages? They were just animals." Nonetheless, a seed was planted.

Shortly after this experience Kathy was getting ready to drive to her group therapy session. "I had decided I wanted to go a different route," she said. "I wanted to stop by a store on my way, so I deliberately left a little early. You know how you can be driving on mental auto-pilot and suddenly you wake up and don't even know how you got wherever it is you've ended up? Well, that happened and I realized I was driving the same route I always drive.

"I stopped at a stop sign and suddenly I heard a big noise like a thud. I looked around and this very large bird had just fallen to the ground. It was on its back in the grass. So I pulled the car over and got out."

A full-grown bald eagle had just flown into power lines and been zapped. As Kathy approached, he struggled to right himself, managing to sit up, but just barely. "He was obviously dazed," Kathy said. "He was the largest eagle I'd ever seen. He had all of the traditional coloring, the white legs and head. He had to be about three feet from head to tail feathers. He was just beautiful."

Kathy was afraid to get too close, conscious of his powerful looking beak and talons. "I looked him over from a distance and didn't see any burn marks or anything. I was concerned and wanted to help him, but I wasn't sure what I could do for him." Although the eagle seemed to gaze around, he was not focusing on anything. Nonetheless, something happened when Kathy looked into his eyes.

"The nearness of that bird really hit me," she said. "His eyes were golden, and my sense at the time, looking into them, was that I was looking into infinity, something sacred. It was incredibly moving. I felt very honored to be so close to this bird."

Because he wasn't focused, Kathy felt he looked right through her, rather than at her. It only added to the sense of the ethereal, one step apart from earthliness.

Kathy talked soothingly to him for awhile, still wondering what to do when a man drove up in a four-wheel drive vehicle. "He said he knew someone who worked at rehabilitating wounded animals. He wrapped the eagle up in his shirt and took him off. The eagle didn't protest at all."

Kathy drove on to her group therapy session feeling strongly impacted. "I knew this experience was something big. I shared it at group but I'm not sure anyone had any idea what I was talking about. At that time, we were all kind of neophytes on this journey of new awarenesses and no one had mentioned the concept of an animal angel yet. I just knew I needed to talk about the eagle."

When she got home she called the Native American leader from the weekend before. He told her some of the qualities of the eagle. What impressed Kathy the most was that the eagle could fly high enough to see the whole picture.

Virtually overnight, Kathy had a paradigm shift. "When I

looked into the eyes of that eagle, I knew it had been sent to me. There was no doubt in my mind that that eagle fell there for me. What I got from it was that God speaks to us in many ways. Angels don't have to be limited to people-like figures with wings who fly around. And all of creation is important, not just humanity. The church's teaching is that man is supreme over all the animals and I couldn't accept that anymore. It wasn't working for me. I was grateful that God sent me this sign. It really helped me expand my awareness of the Creator. Shortly after that, I left the church."

Still searching, Kathy joined the Episcopalian church. For a while, its more liberal attitude felt better to her and she even considered becoming an Episcopalian minister. But it wasn't long before that also felt too restricting.

"Today, not being part of an organized religion almost feels like not having a home," she said. "What felt good and safe about being in the Catholic religion is gone. And sometimes that's sad, but rigidity is what I gave up. So my path now is just trying to be very aware of God everywhere, in all things. I try to be more contemplative. I've learned that being rigid doesn't allow us to hear God's message.

"Once I got out of that paradigm of black and white, right and wrong, I could really listen to and appreciate other people's beliefs and participate in ceremonies, which I could never have done before."

"This whole experience allowed me to open up spiritually. I've been more open to alternative experiences, which I've been doing ever since, without guilt.

"I'm extremely grateful for the Catholic upbringing," Kathy went on. "It gave me a very strong basis and love for God. It just doesn't fit now. I even find Christianity too limiting. I struggle with that because it's so ingrained. I absolutely believe in Jesus and what he taught. But I also believe that God speaks to every person regardless of religion and beliefs. I just can't limit God anymore. I just can't put Him in a box."

"I've watched Kathy struggle and put as much effort and energy into her therapeutic work as anyone I've seen," Michael said. "She's done a lot of work in a lot of areas of her life, but religion was a tough one for her. She was searching for truth and dogma kept getting in her way. She needed an eagle to literally fall out of the sky!"

Bulls are another kind of animal that have played a role in religious worship, including Christian worship, for centuries. Mythology is rife with bull tales, and the bull is one of the symbols of the Zodiac. Taurus the Bull represents solidity, the firmness of the earth and material values. The Brahma bull in particular is a magnificent specimen of bovine beauty.

Sarina and the Bull

Sarina is a woman of Native American descent who was raised within a highly fundamentalist church. As a member, she had been exposed to conflictive belief systems and religious boundaries which, until recently, she hadn't even thought to question. However, exactly one year before this story, she had an experience which first opened the door to new ideas.

At that time, Sarina went through a difficult pregnancy and a dangerous birth. She had been bedridden, bled every two weeks and finally, while undergoing a C-section, died on the operating table. "I knew I was slipping away when I heard them say, 'She's leaving us,' and I crossed over. I saw my own DNA; I saw the light; I knew for a moment that I was divine. But the doctors intervened and I returned to my body and life here on earth.

"When I was well again, I talked to a Native American advisor, and we both agreed that something momentous had happened the night I gave birth."

Still, Sarina wasn't sure where to put this experience. By her fundamental Christian upbringing, women didn't have visions; only men were capable of such communion with God.

Shortly thereafter, Sarina met Michael through a mutual friend. That winter and spring, Sarina worked on personal issues and became exposed to the idea of animals as symbols of something more. "Honestly, I picked it up like a game," she admitted. "I looked at it like a ouija board, but it was very interesting so I dabbled in it through those four months."

One day in April, exactly a year after her near-death experience, Sarina dropped her daughter off at school and began to drive the half-hour trip home. "My year-old son was asleep in his car seat and I was quietly going over my thoughts of the last year," she explained. "It is a comfortable time for me, full of reflection and daydreams. The drive is on a two-lane highway through long, deep pastures and orange groves, broken occasionally with palm trees, scrub or oak trees dripping with moss. I usually spend my time listening to classical music and challenging my thoughts about my childhood religious upbringing, deism, humanism, my place, my relationship with my husband, my children's lives and how they all work in tandem to prevent or propel me in my life. I often get to a place of frustration and denial. Or I get bored with the same repetitions of thoughts and move to designing start-up businesses or making grocery lists."

On this day, however, Sarina began replaying the previous evening's conversation with her husband and Michael. Suddenly, she became aware of birds everywhere, crows, vultures and grackles flying, perched on fences and powerlines. "I was reminded of a passage I had just read in the novel *The Valley of Horses* by Jean M. Auel in which she describes a vision of Mother Earth as the creator of all. At that moment a sense of ecstasy came over me so strongly that I thought I was going to pass out. The skin over my entire body crawled with goose bumps as if I had just stepped into cold water. My hands shook so that I wasn't sure I could hold on to the steering wheel. My heart beat so strongly that I truly felt like it would burst. And my eyesight became so clear I could see even the smallest insect on the leaves of the scrub pine to my right.

"Every animal became a symbol, every blade of grass a metaphor, even the electrical poles on the side of the road, which have always repulsed me, had meaning. I was filled with a sense of love that left my inner and outer body trembling with the magnitude and awe of understanding. I was literally flooded with light. It was exactly what the Bible talks about when Paul couldn't stand up on the road to Damascus. He was prone for three days because he was so blinded by the light. If I could have fully given in to the moment, I'm not sure that I wouldn't have died or at least passed out."

In fact, Sarina was shot back in time to when she lay dead on the operating table. "I thought maybe I was having some kind of *Jacob's Ladder*-type experience and I'd been dead all this time, that this past year had all been some kind of illusion or something."

However, Sarina was driving a car at fifty-five miles per hour down a two-lane road with a baby in the back seat. Frantically, she struggled for control. The first control that popped into her mind was an old teaching. "Instantly that critical voice of my dogmatic religious upbringing jumped in and said, 'No! Not a female.' And I said, 'But...'

Sarina's religion had given her a gift, however. "I'd been taught that if something is true, the burning will be in your heart. If it's not true, you will be confused. Well, it was so clear! Everything was clear. Yet could it be true? Precisely at that moment I turned my head and saw the most magnificent Brahma bull, in a pasture where I had never seen cattle before."

The bull's golden coat stretched taut over his massive forehead and shoulder hump. He radiated warmth and power in the early morning sun. His light, cream-colored breast and legs were strong and purposeful, the muscles relaxing and tightening as he swung his enormous head and rack of horns back and forth, leading his cows down a sandy path through the scrub pines. Suddenly, he swung his massive head and stared straight at Sarina. "He locked eyes with me," Sarina said, still feeling emotional. "It was almost more than I could bear. He was so magnificent and glowing in the morning sun that it almost hurt to look at him. He looked me straight in the eye and I heard the words, 'Yes, it is true! You got it!' "

Somehow, Sarina managed to pull the car over to the side of the road and park. She collapsed, sobbing in a way she still finds hard to explain. "It wasn't fear, it wasn't sadness, it wasn't even joy, it was total release, total acknowledgment of the oneness, of what it all is. I sobbed in a way that was like an orgasm. Suddenly I knew it all; it didn't matter if I'd been raised Catholic or Jewish or Baptist or anything, I got it!"

With an understanding born of what could only be termed enlightenment, Sarina "saw" creation in a way she had never seen it before. "The God of this universe is not one male God sitting in judgment of me with a devil tempting me with evil, it's a being of such wonder with a mate of such beauty that all was in Their image. That the act of creation we share with all animals, plant life and even germs, the entire natural world were His and Her gifts to each other. That pleasure and pain were both gifts and that without one the other could not be appreciated. That perfection was in understanding the relationships between the two sides and the whole, and not in an individual being 'righteous.' There is no religion, or righteousness, in the natural world, but there is creation. And all of it is with a mate, male and female halves…from the tiniest cells to the giant whale."

Hastily, Sarina grabbed paper and pen and scribbled notes, both to capture the feelings of the moment and to reconnect with the physical world. Finally, she felt she could trust herself to finish the drive home. But the universe was not done with her.

"Each moment the feeling threatened to take over again as I saw the truth of the world around me. I saw beautiful white egrets take off in flight toward the azure sky and felt my throat catch and my eyes sting with tears. I saw an old man bent toward the right carrying loaded bags of tin cans down the roadside. This time, instead of pity, I felt overwhelming love and appreciation for the gift of his body bent in labor so that I might enjoy my drive free of roadside debris. I saw a mother driving a beat-up car and instead of feelings of superiority I knew she was a sister and thanked her for her sacrifice. I saw a man speeding past me in a large SUV with a cell phone to his ear and felt compassion for his need to succeed. I felt all these and more. I felt giddy and silly and not sure that I hadn't just lost my mind."

As Sarina continued her drive, she wondered if a physician might treat these symptoms with medicine or if a man of religion might want to exorcise her. "If I told my husband, would he leave me, because it's just too crazy, too out of the norm? Perhaps there was a scientific explanation? I hadn't eaten yet that day, and I had coffee on an empty stomach. Perhaps it was just a moment of hallucination brought on by low blood sugar and caffeine."

Sarina knows better. She has never been so sure of anything in her life.

"My unusual upbringing did leave me open to the idea of visions," she explained, "but I never believed they could come through a female. Of course, in my head I've always fought it. Why not a female? But apparently my heart really did pick up what I was taught because when this happened, I instantly thought this must be from the dark source. That didn't last long!"

Sarina feels that it was the idea of animals being messengers from God that first opened her to seeing more. "I've always been organically tuned in to animals, my pets, my horses. I felt I could talk with them, understand them. But today I partially recognize this as being ego-driven. I personified them. Their symbolism is not in being human; it's in being exactly what they are as the specific animal they are. That's what the vision opened up for me. That's what the bull told me."

Since this experience, every day that Sarina drives her daughter to and from school she has looked for that bull. He has never been in that pasture again.

"The things that have happened since then could take a week to explain," she said, laughing with delight. "The way I've tried to explain it is that it is about accepting that spirituality is different from the dogma of religion. I no longer feel restricted by dogma, both directions, either for or against. But I feel so full of spirituality that I sometimes think I will burst."

Since the time this story happened, Sarina has become more actively involved in her Native American traditions. She has continued to have visions. She feels that she has regular communion with what she calls the Creator. "It's not about revelations or commands," she said, trying to explain the unexplainable, clearly frustrated with the lack of accurate words in her vocabulary. "They're more like affirmations, flooded feelings of 'Yes!' One of the biggest things I've learned is that the Creator is so patient with me."

Sarina is an artist and has been highly inspired in her work ever since her first vision. Several problems with which she had been struggling, have since resolved themselves. She also feels that she can see metaphors and symbolism in such a clear way that she is willing to share her gift with anyone who might be able to use it. "The animals, the light poles, the old man picking up trash, it was all symbolic, it was all whole, it was all One, all exactly as it had been on the operating table when I heard the thoughts of the surgeons rather than their speech," she again tried to explain. Then she gave up. "It just is," she said.

The first time she ever did a reading, she made it clear that this was not about worshipping animals, cards or the interpreter. It was about her being a conduit for whatever the Creator was sending toward the person who had requested the reading. "I became flooded and this person was highly impacted by the reading," Sarina said. "One of the biggest things has been that it really isn't about me. That's really what is so awesome."

"If ever anyone wants to know what it feels like to 'get it,' " Michael said, "Sarina's story will do it. This woman had been listening to the stories, the concept of just accepting herself for who she was the way the animals accept themselves. Awakening really is about acceptance. When you can accept yourself, you start becoming more and more accepting of everything around you."

An awakening is the goal. Some kind of ah-hah experience, some kind of epiphany, it's what we're all looking for. "Sarina saw it all. All of a sudden she was in tune with all the connections of nature. How pure and perfect it all was. How divine!"

"I don't ever try to tell anyone what to believe," Michael went on. "The search for truth is a very personal search. It's different for everyone. Far be it from me to tell anyone that they are doing something wrong by going to church or not going to church. That's not for me to say. But for me, the very fact that we sat down to tell all these stories is a sign of faith."

chapter ten

—◆—

Rites of Passage

When a boy of about five, I caught my first bird and
my father celebrated the event by giving away a horse to
someone else, an old man who could never return the gift.
That was the beginning of my religious training.
— *Standing Bear*

There are many transitions in life. However, perhaps the toughest,
especially in our society, is the transition from "young" to "old."
This occurs at different times for different people, but it always means
a psychological and emotional shift of some kind. Some of us fight it;
some of us accept this state of life more gracefully than others. Some
clearly recognize that they go from being seekers and doers to being
mentors, role models and elders. Unfortunately, that seems to occur
more often in cultures other than our own, cultures in which youth is
not so idealized.

"I heard some wisdom on an old television show that I just
loved and have always remembered," Michael said. "A character said,
'My pappy always said that we get to live two lives: one in which we
learn to live and one in which we get to live.'"

For most of us, the transition from "young" to "old" begins to occur in our late forties or early fifties. Because we're taught that being and looking young is what matters in life and that the older people have lost their value, there is much depression, illness and upheaval in life at this time. "This attitude is strongly influenced by the mass media, which pushes the sales of products to make us young again," Michael said.

Michael remembered an animal show he once saw. Not long ago, a new park opened up in Africa. Because their elephant populations had been decimated, the biologists decided to re-introduce an elephant herd to the park. They went out and chose young, vital, healthy elephants, adolescents and young adults, and set them up as a herd in this new park. They proceeded to tear the park apart. "The elephants were tearing down trees, wreaking havoc everywhere. The biologists were smart enough to recognize that they had done something wrong. They quickly realized there were no elders in the herd, no one to lead, no one to lend stability. They inserted a few elders into the elephant herd and instantly the chaos stopped."

All populations need elders, but elders also need to recognize their own value. Growing older is not something we can change. Accepting this fact allows us to grow into our wisdom years.

Acceptance. Tolerance. Adaptability. That's what growing into maturity, wisdom and "elderhood" means. However, simply reading or saying this does not mean it happens quite so easily. For many of us, there are issues that must be dealt with before we can accept our transition from youth to maturity.

Sometimes biting insects can help "point" out issues with which a person is dealing. Bites often occur along the body's specific meridians of energy. A study of these meridians will often prove that the insect is simply going for the weak spot in the body's defenses, its Achilles heel.

Samantha and the Dragonflies
Samantha is an outgoing, full-of-life fifty-four-year-old woman living and working in southern Florida. She is a park ranger, though she's still not sure how that came to be, as she had few qualifications for the job

when she applied with the park service. Today, she's a happy, productive ranger, but in mid-2002, she almost quit. She owes her continuing employment to dragonflies.

Samantha grew up in Iowa, a far cry from the warmth and quasi-tropical climate of Florida. "I was clumsy and isolated as a child and most of the time I didn't fit in," she said. "But the one thing I remember very strongly was that whenever I went to summer camp, I was happy. I loved being in the woods and how still and quiet everything became. Society and all of its expectations disappeared.

"I particularly remember being in a canoe in the water when I was fifteen or sixteen. The quality of the light filtering through the trees and sparkling on the water is a strong image with me today. And part of that picture includes dragonflies."

That was when Samantha first studied the mythology of dragonflies. "I learned that the iridescent wings of dragonflies were the scales of ancient dragons," she said with a grin. "I've grown up with that fantasy, and with the idea of dragonflies having a strong mythical and contemplative association for me. Wherever I saw them, I became aware of my transition from all the noises in my head about society's expectations, to feeling a part of the earth, a part of nature. Dragonflies have always inspired such feelings in me."

That was also when Samantha decided she wanted to be a camp counselor. "From the time I was about fifteen, that's what I most wanted to be," she said. "But the first summer I was going to pursue it, my parents thought better of it and sent me off as an exchange student to England. Mind you, that was an awesome experience also, but I lost the chance to fulfill my dream of working outdoors."

Samantha grew up and went on to pursue life in an ordinary fashion, working indoors at office jobs. Yet she maintained some far-off sense of connection to dragonflies and to nature. Over the years, she studied Native American ideas, animal medicine and more mythology. Dragonflies, as evidenced in the jewelry in many cultures, have always been symbols of transformation and also of water, particularly clean water.

In 1980, Samantha moved to the Northwest to take care of an aunt, her mother's only sister. For the next twenty years her aunt, and running her own social services business was her life. Then within the first six months of the year 2000, Samantha lost her mother, her aunt and her best friend. The next three years were a time of major transition in her life.

"I came to Florida to visit friends and family," she explained. "And to this day I have yet to go to a big Florida city like Miami or Orlando. I haven't even set foot in Disney World. I chose instead to go to Myakka State Park that first trip, and I fell in love with it. I was in awe. I'd never seen anything like it."

Samantha went back to the Northwest, but within a year made the decision to move to Florida. "Living in the northwest had been my aunt's dream," she said. "Now it was time to find and follow my own dream. My family responsibilities were finished. What's next for me, I wondered."

When she returned to Florida, her first trips were to visit nine different state parks. "I'd just fallen in love with Florida's state parks," she said. "I made it my goal to visit every one of them."

At the time of her move, Samantha had just turned fifty-two and was well aware of what that age meant. "In many cultures it is a time of rites of passage. Fifty-two is four times thirteen; it's when we become the elders, the wise ones. For women, it means we become crones." At the same time, Samantha was indeed going through menopause. She was not feeling especially youthful when at the age of fifty-three, she began trying to find a new job in Florida.

"The businesses I'd always been in were no longer appealing," she said. "I looked into several, but I just couldn't do it. I'd been working indoors since I was a kid. I was ready for something different."

She stumbled onto a job advertisement on the Internet for a state park ranger in southern Florida, where she was living. Instantly she knew that was it.

"Somehow, I talked and wrote my way into this phenomenal job, but I'm not sure how!" she laughed. "I'm out of shape and the last person you'd expect to be a park ranger!"

But her prospective employers saw something in her, because she was hired. When she began working, in February of 2002, her new boss gave her a warning. It was cool in February, he told her, but the summers in southern Florida, with the heat and the mosquitoes, would be challenging, especially for a woman who had spent the last twenty years in the Northwest and virtually all of her life indoors. Her biggest test would come in the summertime, he warned.

However, for Samantha it was challenging right off the bat. The physical work was hard on her older and less-than-conditioned body. She didn't have much knowledge of Florida's unique ecosystem or of basic maintenance, a main ingredient of any park ranger's job. She struggled just to do her job. And then, summer arrived.

"My boss was right! It gets really hot here!" she said. "Really hot!" The job began feeling less and less like a dream come true, and more and more like Dante's version of hell. The rangers at this particular park wear mosquito suits in the summer, full-length nylon jackets with screens over the faces. "Wearing them is like being in an oven," Samantha said grimly. She was still struggling with learning the necessary skills of her new job and that point in by mid-summer, she was faltering.

"I thought maybe I was too old to learn new tricks," she explained. "Maybe I just wasn't cut out for this kind of work. I didn't think I was going to make it."

By sunset that day, she was the only ranger on duty, and gave in to her deteriorating confidence and negative state of mind. Her work shift that day was manning the ranger station and dealing with the public that came to visit. As she went about her job inside the station, Samantha seriously contemplated quitting. It was in this sad, defeated state that she slipped into her nylon suit near the end of her shift. It was dusk, the worst time of day for the mosquitoes. The last of her duties for the day would be to take down the flags, close the gates and shut up shop.

"When I stepped outside, it was as if I walked into another dimension," she remembered, still in awe. In the air above her head, approximately eight feet up, was a thick layer of dragonflies, feasting on mosquitoes. "I knew that Native Americans call dragonflies 'mosquito hawks,'" she went on, "but I'd never seen it manifested so clearly. The whole quality of the light and air shifted with all these thousands of beating iridescent wings over my head.

"Suddenly, the dragonflies started flying right up to me, inches in front of my face. They didn't quite hover, but almost. They'd come right up to me, stop, as if looking at me, and then fly off. Then several bumped into me. I could hear their wings and the sound they made when they bounced off my nylon suit. And I actually heard their message. It wasn't verbal, but I still heard it: 'Wake up! Wake up!' "

Samantha looked around at the cloud of dragonflies encircling her and said to herself, "This is worth it. Being here is worth the hard work."

"I haven't looked back since," she added. "This is how I intend to complete my life's work. I don't think I'll question my decision to become a park ranger again."

Far from questioning, Samantha dove back into her job with all of her innate enthusiasm and love of nature. She began working out, recently entered the Senior Olympics, did well enough to bring home medals in shotput and discus and to qualify for the state finals.

She also proceeded to study dragonflies seriously. "I decided if I was going to live in mosquito heaven, I wanted to know a lot about the critters who feed on mosquitoes!" she laughed. She is in the process of putting together an interpretive talk on dragonflies. Already several other parks have asked her to come give her talk when she's ready. As Samantha has shared her story with others in the park service, she has proven to be an inspiration. Apparently she is not alone in undergoing rites of passage as an older person entering a new job arena. Within Florida's Park Service, she is called the Dragonfly Lady.

"When I think of Samantha's mood that day, I think of stories I've heard of anthropologists and people like Jane Goodall heading out into the jungles to study specific animals," said Michael. "There's a film clip of Goodall in the early days when she was out for weeks, maybe months and hadn't even seen the chimpanzees yet. She's sitting in front of a camera and she's covered with flies. She's crying and having an awful time; she's ready to quit.

"We live in artificial, climate-controlled condos, in cities and offices and houses that have us so far from nature that we forget we *are* nature. But at some point in many people's lives, there comes a switch and they change from being aliens on this planet, living only in a controlled environment, to becoming an integral part of the planet. Something often triggers this.

"I remember one workshop I went to where there were swarms of black flies. My friend and I made the decision to make peace with the black flies, to accept that they, too, were part of creation. We hardly were bitten, but everybody else, though sprayed with repellant, still suffered bites. We tried to explain that it was about accepting that flies are a part of nature, too, and a little blood loss isn't going to hurt anybody. Somehow, we were no longer targeted. I don't know exactly why that happens, but it does. I've seen it too often. A shaman might call it shape-shifting. The flies only attacked people who were in fear and discomfort, but not us.

"Samantha's switch went off and she got the connection," Michael said. "She realized that if she relaxed and settled in, then nature would back off and allow her to succeed."

"In my work over the years, I've begun to recognize that we go from being an adolescent to what I call a sub-adult," Michael said "We stay in this sub-adult period until some kind of outside force breaks down our childhood beliefs and defense mechanisms. This force will be something that so totally overwhelms what we believe that we have to throw it down and start over. It's like Humpty Dumpty and his great fall. He couldn't be put back together the way he was.

"So when we stop living the lives our of our parents and come to grips with the fact that their life plan will not work for us, then we can begin to rebuild our lives in our own ways. We can become what we were born to be; we can become more harmonious with our own moral fiber. We then have a sense of well-being and connection beyond ourselves. When this breakthrough takes place, we become an adult. Historically it's supposed to happen between the ages of thirty-three and thirty-five. I think this is now being delayed because of our resilience, denial and medications. Instead of complete breakdown, people go into this time of turmoil and suffering. They get divorced, have problems with their kids and they suffer. Where mid-life crises used to take a year or two, now they may take as long as ten years. Some people start to take medication and stay medicated the rest of their lives."

One of the rites of passage that occurs later in life is the dramatic change when children leave the nest. Probably the person most impacted by such a change is the mother. At a time in her life when she may be undergoing dramatic physical changes, mood shifts and fears of aging, she also must endure the feeling of not being as needed as she once was, or at least, not in the same way.

Even when the mother understands all of this, it can still be difficult to adjust, accept and let nature take its course. Few human parents are as fiercely protective as mockingbird parents.

Karen, the Mockingbirds and "B"

Karen and her husband Ted are fairly well-adjusted people, happily living new lives together after their children became adults and moved out of their homes. Although they are happy, the adjustment to a childless household has not been easy, at least not for Karen. One of the ways she managed to cope was by turning to nature with unusually observant eyes and through willingness to learn what it was trying to teach. Much of this story came from her habit of journaling, another part of her own attempt to cope with the fears, the losses and the pride of watching her children step out into a potentially hostile, yet beautiful world.

"Our first daughter leaving home wasn't too difficult for me," she offered. "She married the boy she'd dated for ten years, a wonderful boy and they lived close to our home. I got to be there all along the way as she had her babies and they settled into their own lives together. Although it had some rough times, I was able to step back and let my daughter and my son-in-law live their own lives . . . mostly!" she added with a wry grin.

But when their youngest child, Lyndy, graduated from high school, went away to college and began traveling the country with her friends on special school programs and having boyfriend troubles, it was a little harder for Karen not to worry. As her children moved around the country, mother's protective wings didn't seem able to reach far enough.

As she was fretting about her youngest child, Karen was given the gift of watching a bit of drama unfold. This drama helped her understand a little more about how to let beloved things go.

From her favorite chair on the screened porch, Karen watched a pair of mockingbirds build their nest early that summer. "I got a kick out of how they would carry sticks and twigs and moss to this small, high branch that barely seemed capable of maintaining the weight of the birds themselves. I guess they knew what they were doing. It was a safe home, too high for the neighborhood cats and the branch was too small for the larger predator birds to land on."

Karen remembers well a local mockingbird that everyone called Chip when she was growing up. He kept all the nearby cats and dogs bald and cowering during nesting season. So it was with interest that she watched the preparations for a new family of "Chips." Not long after the nest was completed, the babies hatched and Karen and Ted watched as the parents began their frantic trips to and from the nest with caterpillars, dragonflies and other creatures to feed their young.

Karen and Ted also own a black and white cat that had been named BeeBee by the person who had plucked the homeless kitten from the streets. When they took the kitten, Karen and Ted simply called him "B."

His owners well aware of the havoc domestic cats wreak on songbird populations, B was being held captive inside the house until nesting season was over. "One evening, B was sitting in the window frame of the porch meowing at the mockingbird outside," Karen said. "The bird would chirp right back: 'Chip,' 'Yeeeow,' 'Chip' 'Meeeeooowww,' 'CHIP.' The two of them appeared to be carrying on a conversation."

The bird was on the neighbor's roof, about five feet from the porch where B was sitting. The nest branch is about ten feet above the neighbor's roof. "I decided it was time for B, still an overgrown kitten, to get the lesson a little closer at hand, so I let him out."

"Now, this little five-inch bird has chased away red-tailed hawks, fish crows, grackles, starlings, cooper's hawks, and, a couple of days ago, I saw him go after an eagle that landed a little too close to his territory. This was no wimpy little fancy-feathered songster. He was definitely a creature to be reckoned with!"

B moseyed outside looking for lizards to play with, dragonflies to bat or people to sucker up to. What he got was a screech and a dive-bomb attack from a fiery little papa mockingbird that did *not* accept a cat in his neighborhood!

"Well, B is a pretty cool cat—he's not really out there for a meal anyway since everyone within two miles has a food dish out for him and he can eat or sleep in about fifteen different places," Karen laughed. "So he decided to just leave Papa Chip alone."

Unfortunately, the bird did not feel the same. As B rolled back on his belly on the sidewalk, the bird flew down and landed about two feet from his nose. Mama then landed five feet away and both of them proceeded to scream their indignation and demand that this invader leave the territory. B got up at one point, twitched his tail a little in supposed hunter stance. The bird jumped closer, screeched louder and finally bounced up and jabbed B on the head. B jerked back, ears laid down, clearly surprised. The bird prepared to attack again.

Ted, watching from the porch, couldn't stand it any longer. "I have to go save my son!" So B was rescued from the wild mockingbird.

"I realized, as I was watching this scenario, that I was worrying about my daughter on her cross-country trip," Karen admitted. "I was feeling very much like I wanted to go beat up anybody who might try to harm her." Karen also recognized that she was having difficulty relating to this adventuresome, somewhat wild, younger daughter, something that hadn't occurred with her older daughter, who was almost a clone of herself.

The first leg of Lyndy's cross-country trip with friends had been to come visit her mother. After a year away at college, Karen was alarmed by the feeling of unfamiliarity with her own daughter.

"I was struck by our differences in lifestyle, our differences in desires. There were still similarities, but I almost didn't know this young woman, my daughter. Yet when it came time for Lyndy to leave, for the next five weeks of their cross-country trip I felt like the mockingbird—wanting to follow and threaten anyone that might endanger her enjoyment or safety."

As the days wore on, B hated his confinement. One afternoon, he escaped. Instantly, the mockingbirds attacked him. Even as he ran, Karen could see the black fur flying off his rump. B finally turned and raced back for the house. He arrived with less hair than he'd left with.

"I thought things would calm down after B took a beating from that little featherweight," Karen said. "I thought he'd quit trying to escape from the porch and accept his confinement."

As birds will be birds, so cats will be cats. The next day B slipped out the porch door as Karen was leaving for work and would have nothing to do with coming back inside. Karen was going to be late for work so she sent up a quick prayer for peace in the neighborhood and left. "When I came home, B was sprawled at the neighbor's door and it seemed that peace reigned. I breathed a sigh of relief and went inside thinking the wars were over."

However, Karen soon discovered that mockingbirds are not just arrogant, brassy little things as protective adults—they have this attitude before they can fly. She shook her head as she explained. "Here is a nest full of babies with every advantage. Their parents built a fantastic, safe nest in a branch that was unreachable by predators. They are being fed constantly and yet these little stinkers are jumping out of the nest and putting themselves at risk!"

At this stage the baby mockingbirds had their wing feathers, but no tail and no body feathers. "I guess, just because they have wings, the little chicks think they have to use them! They are jumping right out of their nest that is at least twenty-five feet off the ground, perfectly safe, they are totally provided for—yet they jump! What are they jumping into? A thoroughly disgruntled cat that is looking to reclaim his cat-hood! B may not have the courage to take on Papa Chip, but a partially fledged chick is another story.

"I'll bet every parent that has ever gone through teen-hood with a beloved child has imagined a human version of B at the bottom of that long fall from the nest, nails and fangs bared and ready to pounce. The fledgling would have no chance at all."

However, this fledgling mockingbird did have a chance, partially because B was neutered and therefore not the tom he thought he was, and partially because someone else was paying attention. "I heard the screams of the parents and thought they must be tormenting B again, but then I heard the screams of the baby. I tore outside and there was B sitting in front of the baby mockingbird, batting at it with his paws. I know cats, though, and felt that this was a very temporary arrangement. So I grabbed B, tossed him into the house and tried to dodge the mockingbirds as they dove at my head. I placed the baby up on the roof of the cabin and he flew right back to the ground. His wings were good enough for flying down, but not for flying up! As I was trying to figure out the best way to help this dumb little critter who was determined to risk his life, another fledgling came flying down out of the nest, nothing but eiderdown, determination and enough wing feathers to take it away from safety. I sighed, left both fledglings on the ground, walked back into the house and said 'B, you're grounded again.' "

Until the babies got a little more feathered out, which took about a week, B was housebound. "The babies had a chance to learn to fly away from danger," Karen said. "If only all of our children could be so fortunate."

But the cat is somebody's child, too. He proceeded to drive Karen and Ted crazy. They'd walk through the kitchen and he would jump off the refrigerator to attack a passing head. "I'd walk by the computer desk and he'd grab my legs from beneath the desk and scare the dickens out of me. I'd laugh and kick out at him and he would bounce off the bookcases, scattering papers, books and paraphernalia with no sign of any of the grace so inherent in cats. One time, he hit the walls with his back feet and flew across the room, knocking down computer speakers, calculator, chairs." The family's blue-crowned conure, with whom B has had a fairly amiable relationship, began flying all over the house in alarm. B decided to go after the bird, which was obviously the only thing that was any fun to play with. "That cat can jump at least five feet in the air when there is a bird flying overhead!" Karen said.

B finally settled in, but then appeared to be sinking into, in people terms, what could only be called depression. About that time, Karen heard from her wandering daughter. "Lyndy was really sounding down and homesick," Karen remembered. "After speaking to her on the phone my feathers got all ruffled up again—I felt like those blasted mockingbird parents, wanting to protect my young.

"Oh, the mothering genes—do they ever let go? Sometimes I have kicked the kids out of the house and sometimes I absolutely ache because I am no longer able to hug them. A parent's job is to become obsolete. But sometimes, I almost wish I hadn't taken that job.

"A phone call from Lyndy reminded me of my baby mockingbird falling from the nest. But so far the proverbial cat has not been waiting and it looks like she knows how to use her wings. I'm very proud of Lyndy."

Shortly after the last incident, B managed to sneak out of the cabin. He took off across the yard like an escaped convict on his final attempt at freedom, ears flat against his head, a headlong dash," Karen said. "Straight up the nearest oak and he was twenty feet above our heads before we could even get out to the sidewalk."

They knew they were beat so Ted and Karen went back to dinner, keeping their ears peeled for the birds. It didn't take long. This time, Karen panicked when she heard Papa Chip screaming from the neighbor's rooftop. "I dashed outside and there was B with a baby bird in his mouth. After a little dancing around the yard in chase, I grabbed B, threw him into the house and went back to see the baby. There was not a mark on it. Its feathers were damp, but the down was barely ruffled—no blood and no obvious injuries. I cursed out Papa Chip for not keeping his babies in his nest, left the baby sheltered in some shrubbery and went inside to thank Mr. B for being gentle.

"The cat was driving me as crazy as the teenagers used to when they were grounded," Karen explained. "Now I remembered why I didn't ground them very often—I think it was harder on me than it was on them! But thank you, B, for being gentle with that baby. It's funny how, when you least expect it, even the brattiest of kids come through sometimes. Just when you are at wit's end, they show you a little piece of angel.

"Here's to the little piece of angel in all of us and in all of our children," added the mother who finally, after the lessons from the birds and cat, is learning to let her little one fly.

The weekend finally came when the mockingbirds left the property. No protective sounds had been heard, so Karen decided to let B out for a trial run. B went out the door like a bullet. Their neighbors had family, which included two little girls, staying for the week. These girls had seen B through the screen porch door and were dying to meet him. As B rocketed out the door, neighbor-Dad asked if it was okay if his kids "saw" the cat. Of course, Karen said sure.

"These two little pixies, about six and four, followed B all around the cabins with pieces of tickle grass and lovely little giggles," Karen said and smiled, remembering her own little one-time pixies.

"Now here's the weird part that has surprised me over and over again with this animal. He made me a crazy woman for almost two weeks in the house. I really expected that he would have nothing to do with anyone once he managed to escape the house and run around outside once again looking for the birds. But that wasn't his point, evidently. He went and curled around those little girls' legs, delighted them with meows and played with the twigs they presented to him. They were so beautiful out in the yard—two little girls and a wildcat turned into a gentle playmate."

Even as Karen was struggling with letting her own little girl go, two little girls walked right into the lesson.

"I continued to watch B, primarily wanting to make sure that the bird threat was gone and no more babies could be harmed. When the little girls went to bed, B finally took off across the yard jumping imaginary boundaries, throwing himself up trees twenty or thirty feet high and running right back down at the same speed. He put on a wild show! How can a cat jump six feet over something that is not there? He was literally jumping into the air, twisting into contortions, tearing up the sides of cabins, trees, branches and back down again. He was nuts. He looked like he thought he was being chased by some demon.

"Then he came home, and began meowing at the door. Ted and I were on the porch and we looked at each other, both of us wondering why on earth he came home so soon. The only thing we could figure was that he had gotten a little attached to being coddled and spoiled in the house. His newly found freedom was maybe too much for him so he came home just to make sure we were still here."

Karen remembered those same feelings from her own rebellious past, and at last, knew peace. "It's all about love, isn't it? Just knowing it's there. That's what gives our children both the wings to fly and the freedom to return."

"This is a great story," Michael said. "Both birds and cat were teaching each other as well as Karen. She was smart enough to be observant and to apply it to her own situation. She's also clever enough to know that if that cat had been hungry, there'd be no baby bird today.

"Of course, that is the hard part. There is risk in life. Some kids—and some birds—won't make it. We have to be willing to leave our children's destinies up to them and God. It's about making peace with the fact that life includes pain and death."

Michael spends a large chunk of his practice with teens and their parents. It's often the parents who need the counseling though. "Trying to get parents to allow their children to make their own decisions, suffer their own consequences, is tough," he said. "It's been said that the parents' job is to give their children roots, and wings. The roots part isn't usually as difficult as the wings part.

"It is essential that kids be allowed to take risks," Michael continued. "You find a lot of this problem when the father is absent. Mothers are more nurturing and fearful for their children's safety, while the father's role is more about encouraging exploration and teaching how to handle danger, not avoid it.

"Our job as parents is to teach children how to handle danger. The lessons should be age-appropriate. If it's a reasonable problem for a three-year-old to handle, don't step in. Let him or her handle it, and tell your child what you're seeing and where the danger lies. You don't teach your child how to handle danger by avoiding it entirely."

Our next story tells the quintessential tale of a life maturing. It perfectly spells out the whole process of growing out of youthful beliefs and into the maturity not just of age, but of discovering one's own truths. This is the story of a man who violated his own moral fiber and lost himself for a long, long time, yet he is one of the lucky ones who got it. Once the paradigm shifts began, they flowed one after another and every time, he shook his head, let it settle, and got it! He will not spend years trying to understand. His reincarnation is as full of vibrant color as the tiny insect—the dragonfly, again—that helped him through it.

Brad and the Dragonflies

Brad is a good-looking, fun-loving ranch hand in Georgia. He could also be called a ladies man, one of those dashing, charismatic types who like women and whose company the ladies also enjoy. Most of his life, Brad had focused on chasing women. But at the age of fifty-one, he began having serious doubts that the way he'd lived his life was really the way he wanted to continue living.

"I'll be honest," he admitted. "When I was younger, well, actually, up to less than a year ago, I was more concerned with getting laid than anything else. My relationships were all based on that good feeling that comes from being sexual with someone. Something always felt missing but I didn't even know what it was. I didn't know that the pain was in my heart. I just didn't know!"

Today, thanks to the insistent visitations of a dragonfly, Brad has had a major paradigm shift, one that he still finds hard to believe, even as it is happening.

Brad grew up in northeastern Connecticut where he was raised by a very strict and controlling father and a mother who had difficulty being close. He remembers very few good times.

"I think my spirit was pretty battered when I was a kid," he said. "I was beaten with a big leather belt and put down by my old man so many times that I really think I lost my spirit."

As a child, Brad learned to turn off his emotions. "I got to the point that I refused to cry. When I was beaten, I'd just shut down and wouldn't let anyone see how much pain I was in." Brad also remembers that when the beatings would start, he'd grind his teeth. *No one's ever going to know how much pain they cause me,* he remembers thinking.

This became a conditioned response to any tragedy or pain in his life. It was a technique that kept Brad's heart locked up for many, many years. "I didn't realize this response wasn't something everybody did until later in life when I had my own kids. I refused to do to them what had been done to me, and I couldn't believe how free and creative they were compared to me when I was a child. They could express themselves and not be afraid of being knocked down emotionally or physically just for thinking and talking about things." He shakes his head, as though wondering what such a childhood would be like.

Brad never bonded with his mother either. "I was a breech birth and I guess my mother had a hard time having me. Maybe that kept her away from me, I don't know. She often threw things at me when I was just being a kid. I didn't think that I was doing anything wrong."

As he grew up, however, Brad recognized that not everyone felt about their parents the way he did. "I'd see other people attached to and affectionate with their mother or having fun with their father and I couldn't even understand those feelings. Why would they want to spend time with their parents when all I wanted was to get as far away from mine as I could? It wasn't till recently that I've begun to realize that I never learned how to bond with anyone. The desire to do so was driven away by my parents."

Brad often escaped to the outdoors and remembers clearly the fascination of dragonflies even as a kid. "They'd land on my fishing pole and on the sides of the boat and stuff," he said. "I always called them little helicopters."

But Brad didn't focus quite so much on dragonflies then because he had one very close relationship through most of his child-hood. "I was raised Catholic, so of course I grew up believing in angels," he explained. "I really did have an angel with me all the time. I felt its presence right behind my shoulder and it felt like it was always with me and always protecting me."

Brad suddenly became so emotional that he broke off talking about his angel. We came back to it later, after he had regained his composure. "This angel kept me doing good things when I was a kid. I felt it helped me make good decisions. I always trusted that spiritual feeling that would tell me if something was right or wrong and help me make the proper decisions. It was protective and it was my guide." At nighttime, Brad felt the angel wrap its wings about him when he slept. This angel was his only spiritual connection for years.

One day, when Brad was twelve or thirteen, he succumbed to peer pressure instead of heeding his angel's advice. "I was with a friend who kept pushing me to steal something; I don't even remember what. He kept telling me nothing would happen, that we wouldn't get caught."

So Brad stole something. "My friend was right; we didn't get caught and nothing happened on an earthly level. But my angel disappeared, never to return. It really felt like I lost my spirit then," he said. "I knew what I did was wrong and that disconnected my spirit. I haven't connected with anything like that again."

With the loss of his angel and the closing down of his heart, Brad grew into what he thought was adulthood. He married three times, had five children, several different jobs and businesses and was into and out of lots of money along the way. Whenever he could take a break from his many responsibilities, he'd go out drinking and partying. Something was always missing, though. Not surprisingly, growing up didn't seem to make life much better.

"You know, I'd look around at others my age as I was growing and I never felt as mature as they seemed to be." That made him feel insecure. But what kept him going was that although others seemed "mature," they always looked so much older and acted like they were in a rut. "I used to think they just gave up on having a good time in life and I wasn't about to let that happen."

As Brad desperately strove to show others he was having a good life, he equally desperately struggled just to hang on. During his second marriage, at the age of twenty-five, Brad suffered a nervous breakdown and was hospitalized. "My wife was pregnant; I was working several jobs to make ends meet and the mother-in-law kept bringing ex-boyfriends to the house to prove that her daughter had made a bad choice. The whole time they visited, they put me down. I finally couldn't deal with the stress and I just shut down completely." Today, Brad believes it was a good thing, that it might have been far worse had he not succumbed to simply shutting down. But of course, that wasn't his belief then. Then, it was just another of a long string of failures.

At the time of his third divorce, hearing his father ask crudely, "What'sa matter with you, you can't keep a woman?" Brad decided it was time for a major change. He left everything behind and moved to Georgia.

"I was very angry when I moved south," he explained. "I was really hurt by my last divorce. I thought that one was going to be it; I wanted closeness in my life. When my wife found other company, I just went and did the same. By the time I moved down here, I decided it was time to try to evaluate my life, figure things out." Everything hurt.

Nothing made sense. Brad went back to his drinking sprees and chasing after women for a single night of closeness.

One day, Brad met a woman with whom he struck up a friendship. As usual, the attraction felt sexual to him. However, although Brenda gave him enough signals to make him think she too was attracted, she didn't respond sexually. "She told me later that she recognized something in me, like a door about to open, a readiness. She said the feeling was really strong and she thought she had come along to assist in some way. I didn't know what she meant then.

"Every time we'd get together she'd start talking about things I'd never heard of, non-religious but spiritual and energetic types of things. It had me shaking my head, but somehow it was making sense."

She also told him that he was a people person, loved to be around people and that it was himself he was most hurting by shutting his heart down. She told him that his running around and partying was a shield against potential hurt. These were things he'd never thought of before. But they too made sense. Sure enough, some door seemed to open. "Something kind of happened to my heart," he explained, "but it was so new, I didn't even know how to define it. I thought I was just falling in love."

The first changes were subtle. He thought he was just holding back sexually until she was ready. He eagerly awaited a more physical response from her. "Not being sexually active with Brenda right away was the best thing that's ever happened to me, at this point in my life," he said, still a little mystified. As little as a year ago, he never dreamed he'd be saying such a thing. "I doubt we'd be friends today if we'd been sexual first."

At that point in time, however, he was hoping for more, still gently pushing Brenda for a sexual, and possibly, a love relationship. It was the only familiar foundation he had.

One day, while on the job at the farm where he worked, Brad was trying to jerk the pin out of the shaft hook-up of a tree cutter so that he could hook it up to the tractor. The tool hadn't been used in some time and the pin seemed to be jammed as well as covered with dirt or dried mud of some kind. With one final jerk, the shaft fell down, revealing a hornet's nest and a horde of angry hornets.

Brad leaped back into his truck and waited a while for the angry hornets to leave. At last, thinking it was safe, he went back to the implement to finish the job. One pin remained and as he struggled with it, several more hornets buzzed angrily out of the end of the shaft. "But this time, two dragonflies suddenly showed up and started chasing the hornets back into the shaft. At first I couldn't believe it; I thought I was imagining it. But as I kept fighting the pin and watching, there was no doubt these two little helicopters were keeping the hornets away from me. It gave me just enough time to pull that last pin out and then I ran for the truck again. Once I was safe inside, the dragonflies disappeared."

Inside the truck, Brad sat there, thinking about it. "I had no clue what had just happened. But I had this strange sensation that they had just protected me, that they were taking care of me. It was really amazing!"

The next time a dragonfly made its presence known, Brad had gone to visit Brenda. At the end of the visit, he headed back to his truck. As he raised his hand to open the door, a dragonfly suddenly landed on his finger. Startled, he stood for a moment, just staring at it. When finally it flew off, he turned to his friend who was laughing with delight and asked her what that was all about. "She was grinning and told me that it was about transition," he said. "I asked her what the hell transition was. I was kind of shook up by the thing. There were too many weird things happening! And she said it meant I was changing."

He then told her about the interlude just days earlier when the dragonflies had seemed to protect him. "Brenda said she thought the dragonflies were here to support me becoming a new Brad or finding the old Brad that got lost somewhere along the way."

Brenda told him some of the meanings the dragonfly has had over the millennia. He was astounded at how many ways it seemed to fit his life. He'd never even dreamed anything like this before.

"At that time, I didn't really think I was changing that much," he said, "But now, when I look back on it, I definitely was. It has definitely been a transition."

Suddenly, Brad began watching the world around him with eyes wide open. "I think because of the enlightenment and the new awarenesses I've learned from Brenda, and because these damn dragonflies are all over the place, I can't help but look at things differently! No kidding, they're everywhere; I see them constantly. It really got me thinking."

But for a while he found it hard to believe that dragonflies could care about him. As they continuously "bugged" him, he asked in exasperation, "What are these damn helicopters doing?" Yet he was fascinated with their apparent protection of him.

When Brad had a spiritual astrologer do a reading for him and she told him that he always had dragonfly medicine in his life, but that it was particularly strong for him right now, he finally gave up fighting it. "She told me so many other things that were true about me that I couldn't doubt that part anymore," he explained.

Suddenly, a different type of woman was popping up in Brad's life. "The last few months there have been several women that I think these damn dragonflies have turned me onto. These people have helped me realize a lot of things in life. I've grown into looking for more of a mental and heart connection with women. I always thought that was the correct way to do things. I always thought I was being a loving and good person. I never realized I didn't know how!

"And I haven't been sexual with any of them!" he burst out. "I've actually gotten to know these women and I really like it. Every one of them is different, but what they have in common is that they are intellectually and spiritually on a different plane from people I've associated with in the past. They all seem to have God in their lives. And I'm really enjoying their company. These are people who have helped me find my real self again. I'm finding out who I am. I feel very emotional and very spiritual with these people and that's a new feeling for me. I really enjoy listening to my own spirit." Suddenly he stopped speaking and gestured with his hand. "Geez, look at them now!"

We were in his truck as we were conducting this interview, making the rounds of the ranch where he works. As he spoke those last words, suddenly dragonflies were all around us, even flying through the cab. "See?" he said. "They're everywhere!"

Today, when Brad begins to grind his teeth he recognizes it as a signal that he is afraid of some emotional pain. Often it is a hurt of which he was previously unaware. "As soon as I realize it, I open up and let it go. The grinding only lasts a second now. I'm all done with holding that stuff in."

Indeed, Brad gets emotional very easily, a new phenomena that has taken some getting used to. "Brenda says it's the swing of the pendulum, because I've held so much in all these years. Eventually I won't be quite this emotional." He hesitates thoughtfully. "Someday though, I really would like to cry and be held by someone who cares."

Brad has noticed another effect the dragonflies have had on his life. "I noticed recently that when I have a decision to make, where one choice would make me a better person than the other, the dragonflies appear and start flying all around me. It's as if they're trying to influence me into doing the correct thing. And it's happening, I don't make any poor decisions when they're flying around me anymore.

As an example, Brad and another ranch hand were riding around the farm looking for lost cattle. They began talking about hitting a bar after work for a few beers. "I was in a quandary about whether I really wanted to have beer or not. My head was telling me not to go get drunk and crazy. But that other, old side of me said, 'Bullshit! I'm going to go do whatever I want to do!'

"Well, I've never seen so many damn dragonflies in my life! I swear to God, they were everywhere, like you've heard of flocks of blackbirds blacking out the sky? I took that to mean skip the beer. So we went out, but we both had non-alcoholic beer and we had a great time!

"I think what I'm learning is to listen to my inner, spiritual part, to go with the flow so to speak," Brad explained. "If something feels right, or I tell someone about it, or even heed it myself, that is part of the transition that I see in myself. I think I may be growing..." Brad burst out laughing, "...into an adult, finally."

"It doesn't mean I don't like to have a good time," he hastens to add. "Maybe I'm just finding more responsible ways of having fun."

And still there is more. "I've been doing weird things lately," he said, shaking his head. "Like, I've been singing songs from when I was young. Lately, I've started going out at sunrise and standing there with my arms and hands wide open to the sun. Today while I was standing there, I said, 'You do with me what you need.'" He shook his head in amazement.

"I think I've changed into a better person," he said, "Because I've been through so much in my life, I think some things blow over me easier than other guys who are out there having heart attacks. But now,

I think the dragonflies have helped me find my spirit again. I'm aware of a connection to something bigger and greater than me. That someone or something cares enough to send these dragonflies around is a pretty big thing. I'm really so much more aware now, of everything, when they come around."

"So maybe my bad times are over, and in this latter part of my life, I'm going into a new beginning, a metamorphosis."

As Brad was reciting the exciting new changes in his life: opening his heart; opening his eyes; finding his spirit again and feeling that he had guidance and protection, suddenly he looked over at me. "Whoa! Those are the things my angel used to do," he gasped. "I never thought of that. My angel's back!"

A flicker of uncertainty flashed in his eyes. "What if it doesn't want me? What if it doesn't stay?"

A dragonfly flew up to the windshield and seemed to hover a moment. Brad heaved an audible sigh and smiled, a shining glow radiating over his face.

Change is difficult for all of us, but transitions are inevitable in life, whether from child to teenager, teen to adult, young to old. How fortunate we are to have animal angels teach and guide us through these sometimes very difficult rites of passage.

chapter eleven

Death

There is no death, only a change of worlds.
—*Chief Seattle*

As we sat down to write this portion of the book, a friend of Charlene's, whose father had been in the hospital for several days wrote her an e-mail message letting Charlene know that his father had crossed over. He knew nothing about this book, but part of the message, which went out to his many supportive friends was, "Dad's little dog, which doted on him, crossed over the day before he did. I know he went first to find Mom and to be able to meet Dad on the other side."

Death is not an easy subject to discuss, nor an easy time for those who must witness the passing of loved ones or for those who must face their own death. The stories which follow show that even at such hard times, we are surrounded with love.

Al and "Angel"

Caroline, Al's daughter, is a mother of two living in south Florida. Al and Caroline's mother, Gloria, were in their seventies and lived near Caroline. When they had first gotten their cockatiel from a breeder years earlier, they named it Sunny. Upon discovering the bird was female, Al changed her name to Tootie. Tootie was on Al's shoulder nearly every waking hour.

"Tootie was really special to him," Caroline said. "When Tootie was ready to lay eggs, she would start squawking. Even if it was the middle of the night, Daddy would get up, take her out of the cage and she would get on the floor and walk into the closet. If Daddy wasn't following her, she would turn around and call him. She wanted him with her when she laid her eggs. It was really an incredible relationship."

Tootie had been a treasured member of the family for about eight years when an accident happened. Gloria stepped outside to speak to Al about something, inadvertently leaving the door cracked open. Tootie flew out.

"She was horrified when the bird flew away," Caroline said. "They both were devastated. They lived across the street from a school with a great big schoolyard and Tootie took off toward the school. Frantic, Mother called me, so I left work to come help them. Just before I got there, Mother tripped in the schoolyard and fell. She went back to the house while Daddy and I walked and called for the bird. Daddy told me that Mother was so devastated that he was trying to be strong in front of her. But when we were alone, he cried. It was quite traumatic."

Al put on a brave front back in the house, because he didn't want Gloria to feel badly. Of course, she felt terribly anyway. They never found the beloved bird. Tootie's breeders, who were also friends, wanted to give Al another bird, but he would not accept it. His heart was broken and he was afraid to lose another beloved pet. Over the next couple of years no amount of coaxing by Gloria or offers from the breeders changed his mind.

On December 8, 1996, Al's bride of fifty-six years died. Caroline's brother flew down to stay with his father through the funeral. He was scheduled to leave the following Saturday, then Al would be alone. Both siblings were worried about their father and how he would handle living by himself for the first time.

"Late that Friday afternoon I was sitting at my kitchen counter paying bills," Caroline said, "and I heard this bird just chirp, chirp, chirping. It stopped and then it started again. The bird was obviously trying to get my attention, almost frantically. I walked out on my porch, and I looked over at my pool and a pied cockatiel was sitting on the deck by the pool."

Certain it would fly away, Caroline walked out of the porch toward it. "I squatted down, put my hand out and the bird jumped on it. I walked into the screen porch, my heart beating ninety miles an hour and I put it on the table. I couldn't believe this. I have an outside cat and an inside cat. And the bird had been screaming!"

Caroline ran to the phone, called her father and said, "Daddy, mother's sent you a bird." Reminiscing, she says, "Of course he thought I was nutty as a fruitcake. I tried to tell him what happened and asked Dad if he still had Tootie's cage. I finally got my brother on the phone and told him the story. He said they'd be right over.

"My brother went up into the attic, got Tootie's old cage and they drove to my house. Daddy walked over to the bird on the table and put out his hand. The bird got onto his hand, walked up his arm, got on his shoulder, kissed him on his cheek and acted like it had been his bird forever.

"My brother took me off to the side and asked, 'Where did you buy the bird?' I said, 'I swear to you, the bird just came.' It was the most incredible thing I've ever seen. There's just no doubt in my mind that my mother sent that bird because Daddy was going to be alone."

Al agreed the bird had been sent by Gloria and named it Angel.

"You know," Caroline said. "You always say, 'I wish there was a sign that she's okay?' We got our sign."

Today Al is eighty years old and has had carotid artery surgery. He and Angel now live in an assisted living facility. Al's memory is fixated on the past and Angel is usually called Tootie. "Angel/Tootie is in the activity room and everyone in the facility loves that bird," Caroline said. "She really belongs to everyone there, though Daddy doesn't think so! All those folks stop to talk to Angel. He's really bringing a lot of joy to a lot of lives."

Many of the people who come in to do therapy with Michael are coming because someone is their life is dying, has died or they themselves are diagnosed with a fatal disease. This is not an easy subject with which to deal. Our society has not raised us with the tools to assist in someone else's death or to prepare for our own.

"Our culture is so afraid of death," Michael said. "Being afraid of death makes us ready and willing consumers. We buy lots of things and indulge in lots of pastimes, much of it to take our minds off our impending death. We want to feel we have power or control over death."

Sometimes we can even convince ourselves that death is not real. We know it occurs; we know we aren't likely to escape it, but we would rather think of something else for now. Yet, in most indigenous cultures, death is discussed, planned for, accepted as a natural part of life. In some cultures, old people even choose their own times and methods of death.

Currently in our society, however, there is a shift occurring. Many stories have been written about near-death experiences, when people momentarily have crossed over only to return with tales of bliss, comforting light and feelings of overwhelming, unconditional love. More and more people are beginning to realize that in fact, death is only a change.

Although many cultures consider death only a stage, a stage that is often heralded by animals, some European cultures long have thought of the owl as the devil or, like the black cat, the companion of evil witches. Its silent flight, thanks to special feathers, its large nocturnal eyes and its ability to swivel its head almost 360 degrees has contributed to the long string of superstitious beliefs.

In Native American traditions, however, the owl is a major symbol of change. Although some cultures shun owl medicine because they fear the death it symbolizes, other cultures revere the owl for the same reason. They recognize that the owl only symbolizes change, a cross-over. Often, when an owl comes, it does mean death, but it doesn't have to mean physical death. It can mean the death of an idea, a lifestyle, an outgrown truth.

"There is a reason for the beliefs," Michael said, "The owl really does seem to come into a person's life when something big is about to happen, a change is about to occur. It's just too bad that negative connotations have so often been attached to it. I've got story after story about the owl representing death. Not necessarily physical death, but the death of something."

When something is about to die, it also means something is about to be born.

Peggy and the Owl

Peggy learned what owls were all about long before she met Michael and long before she began to study Native American traditions. Peggy is a tall, statuesque blonde. A self-admitted city girl with no knowledge of country life before Michael entered her life, she had no pre-conceptions to prepare her for what happened when her father died.

"I was in Chicago caring for my father who was dying of cancer and I knew he didn't have much longer to live," she began her story. "I was a pediatric nurse and I'd taken a leave of absence from my job. I had come down to stay with him around the clock. I'd been there about a week and he was semi-comatose. It was tough. My mom was in pretty bad shape and my grandparents and family would come in and out, taking turns sitting with him. But it had gotten to where we knew it would happen any time."

Peggy arose at dawn on a cold February morning, and sat in her father's favorite chair looking through a window into his rose garden. The chair was within eighteen inches of the window. "There were a couple of feet of snow on the ground and the dormant rose bushes were sticking out with white snow all over them. I was sitting there with my tea cup in hand thinking about my father. I looked away, then looked back at the window and right there on the window sill, looking in at me, was a giant, barred owl.

"We stared and stared at each other and I started to cry, because I knew that owl was bringing a message that my father was going to die. I don't know how I knew that, but I did. We sat there for the longest time staring at each other. I lost all track of time. It might have been ten minutes; it might have been thirty minutes. I became filled with awe at the beauty of the owl and a sense of peace filled me. I knew my father was going to be in a good place. It was okay that he was going to die."

Peggy finally broke the spell because she wanted to share this new knowledge with her grandfather. She turned away from the window, called softly for her grandfather, turned back and the owl was gone. Within the hour, her father died.

"That owl was my messenger," she said. "I needed that. As much as I didn't want my father to die, I knew he'd all be all right. It gave me great peace."

Peggy tried to convey this sense of peace to the rest of her family members, who were in deep despair. Though she feels her grandfather might have understood a little of what she was trying to explain, it was only she who truly received the message of the owl.

"When the owl came it was a reminder to me that God's still hanging around," she said.

"In times of grief, a person's defenses are down," Michael said. "When Peggy's defenses went down, she was more able to absorb the lesson of that moment. For some reason, Peggy may have been more open to receiving the message of the owl than others in her family. The value in understanding what the owl is about is that perhaps it can be shared with one more person."

"Oh, I got it immediately!" Peggy agreed. "When it was all over I went in the other room and started talking about it with my grandfather. I don't know if I was coherent enough for anyone to pay attention."

It impacted Peggy, however. It may have assisted in the opening of one more door, just enough to let someone completely outside her "normal" frame of reference enter her life several years later, and then to pursue the study of Native American beliefs about animals and their messages.

Michael has seen the light twice in his life. He remembers most of all the euphoria of his near-death experiences. Although he has no desire to die before his time and he still fears some methods of dying, he lives his life unafraid of death itself.

"One of the biggest issues people need to deal with is their war with death. When people come in angry, bitter and fearful, we help them to deal with those feelings. They are normal, healthy feelings, but most people don't know what to do with them. They think it's wrong to be angry with God. So our first job is to help people get through those kinds of feelings and understand that God understands. And we also help people fight for life with every fiber of their being. But there comes a time when we know it is time to cross over. When that comes, it helps to know that death is not the end. The body is finite, the soul is not. We believe that the soul is going to be reborn into another existence. Born into what, we may not know, but too many of us have had glimpses of the other side not to know for certain that death is only a change."

Patti and the Owl

Over ten years ago, Patti, a slender, auburn-haired homemaker and mother of two, attended a workshop where she first met Michael. She can't remember why it was she went to a therapeutic workshop then, but during the course of that weekend, she learned about the idea of animals and Native American beliefs in the symbolism of specific animals. When she returned home, she bought Ted Andrew's *Animal Speak* book and has been using it in her life ever since. She considers it the most important thing that came out of the workshop. Recently, it came in handy at a crucial time in her life.

"I have always been very close to my husband's grandmother," Patti explained. "I used to call her Grand Ma-Ma and looked forward to her visits. She would stay with us for a month every year until she became too ill to travel. I always loved those times she stayed with us."

At ninety-nine years of age, after a long and rich life, Grand Ma-Ma passed away. Patti and her husband attended the funeral in Wisconsin, then returned home. "That first night back home, I was awakened by a noise in the middle of the night," Patti said. "That in itself is pretty phenomenal since I sleep through everything except my children crying out."

Patti continued to hear this strange noise, so she got up to investigate. She walked to the other side of the house and opened a window to look out. She saw nothing. "All of a sudden, I knew without even seeing it that it was an owl outside my bedroom window," she said. She walked back into her bedroom, opened that window and looked out into the moonlit sky. Still she could see nothing. But she heard it.

"I realized I'd never heard an owl in all my years of living there," she said. "I didn't know what an owl would sound like, but I knew that's what it was." Immediately she knew that the owl meant something, that it was bringing her a message. Patti went downstairs to look up the meaning of owl.

"I stopped short at the sentence, 'Owls have been thought to be the reincarnation of the dead.' I immediately understood that this was Grand Ma-Ma coming to say hello and I was very excited to tell the family about it. When I shared the story with my sister-in-law the next day, she said, 'Of course she'd come to you, who else would understand or know it was her?' "

This experience happened to Patti at a time when she was just getting onto what she considered a spiritual path. It was extremely affirming and she continues to use the animal books in her daily life.

Death is only a change. It is part of the path of life. Here and there some people are opening up enough to realize that in fact, while we may not be able to control or stop death from occurring, we do have a great deal of choice when it comes to our own deaths. Whether because of intuition or training, more people today are choosing to die as honorably and as lovingly as they were able to live. The following story is one of the most beautiful I have ever heard and shows what dying can be like.

This is a story about people who recognized that it was time to work with death rather than fight it. It is also an example of how many angels there are to assist and ease the load when we are open to their presence, their very existence. This is the other side of the story; this is how it can be…

Merry and the Universe

In February of 1993, Merry, a slim, attractive blonde who runs a Montessori school, received a call from a friend of her mother's inform-ing her that her mother had been taken to the hospital after displaying severe flu-like symptoms. Merry immediately picked up her seven-year-old son and drove the two hours to the hospital. At first, she wasn't very concerned, and after a week of testing, the doctors could find nothing wrong with her mother.

On Valentine's Day, a Sunday, Merry's mother, Lorry, called from the hospital and asked Merry to come and take off her wedding and engagement rings and take them back to her home where Merry had stayed for the weekend. "I was still busily doing my mother and teacher thing and I was not really focused on this illness being serious. When my mother wanted me to take her rings, I felt a pang. She'd never taken them off."

Lorry and her husband Mike had been close through all fifty-one years of their marriage. It had been love at first sight and that never changed. Mike had died a couple of years earlier, but still Lorry had never removed her rings.

Refusing to accept the situation, Merry was up bright and early the next morning, her head full of school conferences and meetings, coffee cup in hand, preparing to head out the door for the long drive back to home and workday. Her mother was scheduled to be released from the hospital that morning.

"I looked out the sliding glass door into the screened room around my mother's pool and there, sitting on the edge of the pool, was a mourning dove," Merry said. "At that time, I had always thought it was 'morning dove.' It wasn't until after this incident I found out the spelling was 'mourning.' "

The pool area was completely screened in. How the bird had gotten in was a mystery. Merry retrieved a towel and stepped through the glass doors, intending to set the dove free. Immediately, it flew to a plant stand and hid behind it. "I took the towel and dropped it down between the screen and plant stand over the dove," Merry said, "but the dove immediately scooted out from under the towel, then sat there looking up at me. I bent down and picked it up, I cradled the bird between my palms and stroked its head with my thumbs, talking to it, reassuring it. I carried it to the door and outside to a blossoming nectarine tree which I had given my dad just before he died. I set the bird under the tree and it flew off. As it did, I suddenly realized I was being told to let my mother go."

Before Merry could return to her own home, she was called back to the hospital. Her mother refused to be discharged. Since she was still having stomach cramps, the doctor decided to run a few more tests. Merry wavered between the need to return to her school and her mother's needs. Her mother told her to go on, but not before she said, "You know, I think I'm ready for your father to come get me and I think he'll come in a golf cart covered with roses and hearts."

Merry returned to school to find the parents of her students had covered her desk with heart-shaped Valentine candy. She then checked her messages and found that the doctor had called and needed her back at the hospital. They had discovered a hole in her mother's colon. She had peritonitis and surgery was an immediate necessity. Merry quickly made arrangements for someone to watch her son, dog and school, then packed and drove right back to the hospital.

When Merry walked in to the I.C.U. the doctor informed her that they'd nearly lost Lorry on the operating table. They had removed a liter of bile, performed a colostomy and expected her to recover, but she would require a few weeks in intensive care. He also warned her that her mother was on a ventilator. She weighed only eighty-eight pounds.

At that point they would only allow ten-minute visits. Lorry could not talk because of the tube down her throat. They devised a method of communication using blinks of the eye and hand squeezes. A friendly nurse allowed Merry to spend more than the permissible time with her mother. Merry called all her siblings. Her sister and one brother made immediate plans to come. Her other brother wasn't so sure. "I called him three times," Merry said, "but Biff had a hard time believing that this was serious. I know mother held on the seventy-two hours she lasted partly because she and he had unfinished business."

Death was not a taboo subject in their household. Earlier, Merry and her siblings had discussed with their mother how she wanted to die: in a hospital or home, with or without someone holding her hand, on drugs or not, what kind of music. "We really had mapped it out as well as you can," Merry said. "So I hardly left her side now."

Merry sat with her mother for hours, holding her hand, while the eerie sound of the ventilator breathing for Lorry continued, Merry told stories, sang songs. "I sang songs like 'Swing Low Sweet Chariot' and made up lyrics to it about all of our friends and family who had already gone to the other side. It made my mother laugh. And I sang lullabies to her that she used to sing to me."

Merry credits much of her openness to alternative ideas of healing and schooling to her mother, the surprisingly liberal-minded wife of a Navy Rear Admiral. "My mother actually learned to read palms at an early age. I think that experience opened her to other possibilities." Merry lived all over the world because of her father's work and in the seventies she was a full-blown flower child, traveling, studying herbs, living in a commune.

While her siblings thought Merry was too far out, Lorry patiently went along with almost anything Merry brought back home. "I'd talk her into practicing astral travel with me, doing breath exercises. Once when she was having gall bladder problems, I convinced her to white light her gall bladder and she went back and they couldn't find anything wrong with it anymore. She always trusted me and did anything I wanted her to try. So the week before, while we sat day after day at that bedside, I'd say, 'Hey Mom, let's try a practice flight, okay?' And we'd do breath relaxation exercises."

At these times, Merry would invite her mother to fly out of the room, up over the roof and to her own house to see Duke, her poodle. "When the pain hit, she'd jerk back into her body again and I'd say, 'Oh, you're back,' and reassure her."

The hospital was on a causeway over a river, just a street away from Lorry's own house. The entrance to the canal was visible from her hospital room. They'd been told dolphins often came into the canal and Merry and her son, when he was there, took turns watching for them. But the dolphins had remained elusive.

Her older sister arrived. "That morning, I was sitting in the ICU waiting room while my sister was in with my mother. A pair of dolphins swam right by the window. They headed straight to the window off my mother's room and stayed there playing. I went in and told my mother they were out there and described them to her. I had brought my animal medicine cards book with me so I told her what the dolphins meant. 'The dolphin speaks to us of the breath of life, the only thing humans cannot go without for more than a few minutes. ...Within the breath we encounter the rhythm of energy that all life emits. In changing the rate or rhythmic texture of our breath, we can tap into any other life form or creature. This is a very easy way to connect with divine energy coming from the Great Spirit as well as with your own personal rhythms.'"

The text went on to describe how a dolphin breathes: it dives holding its breath, then blows hard when it surfaces. "We can use this same technique to pull the stopper on our tensions and create total relaxation. This is a good exercise to use before entering the silence." The passage also spoke of the legend of the moon inviting a dolphin to learn her rhythms and breathe in a new way in order to enter the dreamtime.

With that reading, Merry suddenly realized that she was being told to help her mother by using breathing exercises for birthing, which she had learned years earlier. That afternoon, the doctor wanted to remove Lorry from the ventilator, but if she didn't do well, he would put her back on it. Merry asked her mother. "If anything happens, do you want the doctor to re-ventilate you?" Lorry frantically shook her head, "No!"

"As the day progressed, everything seemed to slow down and move into slow motion," Merry said. "I felt that everything was happening at exactly the right time, in the right way and for the right reasons. Nothing mattered but the moment."

Merry and her sister waited outside the room anxiously. Time went by. Merry's knotted stomach told her that all was not well. Finally, she insisted she must go back to her mother. "We had promised we'd be with her when she died." The nurse was convinced and talked the doctor into letting them in. Lorry was not doing well. About that time, Merry's brother Biff arrived. He waited outside while his sisters went in.

Lorry was failing, but with the entrance of her daughters, her vital signs improved. Her mother's first words in days were, "That's better." Merry feels that part of this return was so that her mother and Biff could resolve their differences. Although Biff remained uncomfortable with the idea of his mother dying, Lorry and her son had their time together.

The weather grew dark and misty. Merry described to Lorry what she saw through the window, the sailboat slowly passing by, a graceful white silhouette against the stormy gray with sails billowing, then luffing and finally, passing silently into the fog. It began to rain heavily.

Merry, her brother and sister held hands around the bed and prayed together, a longtime family ritual. Merry's other brother was caught in a snowstorm, unable to get there. But they held the phone to her mother's ear so that she could hear her fourth child say his good-byes. The nurse, a wonderfully sensitive woman who let the family do more than she was "supposed to," wanted to give their mother something for the pain. "Just enough to knock the edge off," Merry insisted, "not enough to knock her out. She needs to know what's going on." She explained the situation to her mother and Lorry agreed with her daughter completely.

Suddenly, Lorry grabbed Biff's hand and cried out, "Let me go! Help me go!"

Biff was having a tough time. He still was not ready for her to go. Merry, realizing her mother's distress, crawled into bed with her and began stroking her hair and soothing her. She then explained exactly what the doctor had told her.

"Mom," she said gently. "Your kidneys will stop first, then your heart will probably begin to cramp. What I'm going to do is be your mid-wife. I'm going to help you be reborn to the other side. Whenever your heart squeezes or you feel cramping, you squeeze my hand hard and I'll breathe with you through it. Send me your pain. Are you comfortable with that?" Her mother nodded her assent.

With her brother holding one hand and her sister near the bed, Merry began to breathe with her mother. Willingly, Lorry held tightly to her hand and breathed with her, breath for breath.

"I lost track of time," Merry said. "It's only because my sister kept track that I found out later I was with my mother like that for two and a half hours, which is a normal, healthy birth time. I mirrored every breath she took. I didn't try to make her breathe in any special way, I just breathed with her. When she made "Ahhhh…" sounds, I made the same sounds. Our breathing became so matched, so alike that I felt the two of us became one.

"Then I said, 'Are you ready to call God, Mom?' She nodded

and together we began saying with each exhalation, "God… God…"

"I could see through her eyes, feel with her, I knew her every thought. I fell into a place of love with her. We were both enveloped in an overwhelming, unconditional love. Her eyes lost their bloodshot look and became wide and crystal clear. They were the eyes of a new-born baby. She looked at me with this look of infinite understanding and knowing. Then she looked up and saw something.

"I said, 'Mom, you're almost there. Go to the light, Mom. Someone is waiting for you.'"

Her breathing changed and shortened as the air began to leave her lungs. With every chopped breath Merry and her mother made the "ah," sound into "amen, amen, amen."

"The light and the love surrounded us both," Merry said, "I felt it with her. And I felt her go."

It was later that her brother shared with his sisters that just before she died, he had finally prayed. "I hadn't asked my father for any-thing since I was eighteen," he said. "But I asked him to come for her now. I was ready to release her."

Their other brother, stuck in a car and trying to get to the air-port, looked up at the sky at that moment and saw a shooting star. He said, "Bye, Mom, have a great trip," without any question of what the sign meant. "This is my Green Beret brother who always pooh-poohed me and my 'signs,'" Merry laughed.

The nurse allowed the three siblings time to grieve; then they went back to Lorry's house to have a drink and indulge in the "Irish wake" their mother had requested. Their other brother finally arrived and for hours they shared and healed as they had not in years. "Green Beret" brother got up at one point and went outside, then came run-ning back in, calling for them all to come out.

"There's always one or two pelicans on the canal," Merry said, "But now there was a whole flock of pelicans. They were everywhere. But there were two in particular doing a kind of mating dance. For fif-teen minutes they dove into the water, then rose high into the air, dove and rose, each exactly mirroring the other in the most beautifully syn-chronistic thing I have ever seen. And I've lived near the water for fif-teen years."

The same brother said in awe, "It's Mom and Dad. They're

back together and letting us know it."

During the memorial service, a friend slipped Merry a poem she thought might help. It was "A Parable of Immortality," in which Henry Van Dyke described perfectly the sailboat Merry had seen outside her mother's window as a metaphor for crossing over with loving hands sending it from one side of the fog to the reception of loving hands on the other.

Still it was not over. The next morning, when her siblings were packing to return to their respective homes, they saw something Merry had never seen. Her sister yelled for them to come outside. Instead of the usual one or two birds patrolling the canal, every kind of water bird that exists in Florida had gathered, whole flocks of herons, wood ducks, cormorants, anhingas, egrets and cranes, brown and white pelicans, flying, swimming and circling in a cacophony of sound and color against the backdrop of the water. In clouds they swooped down the canal and clustered about the house. "Wow!" said Merry's sister. "Mom and Dad are really giving us a sendoff!"

Being a full and loving participant instead of a passive, helpless observer to a loved one's death not only makes it easier for the one crossing over, but uplifts forever the ones left behind.

"I was actually high for days afterward," Merry said. "It had been such an incredible experience. With all my training, I never dreamed I would use my breath exercises to help someone die. Without the dolphins, I might not have thought of it."

Merry shared her experience with friends and wrote it up for a school paper. Rarely did the listener's eyes remain dry as her rendition was read. "I thank God that I was open enough and lucky enough to be able to receive all those signs," she said. "Sometimes it's still hard to believe. Everything was so in sync, so slowed down. I was completely in the moment. I remember afterwards walking through her garden and smelling a rose as if I was smelling it for the first time. I felt so blessed."

God, the Great Mystery, the Universe, sends us messages constantly, asking only that we receive. To do that we must be open, believe in the possibilities and accept the true grace and love which surround us constantly in this very credible world, this very credible Creation. All of it is a gift. We don't even have to ask, merely accept. And animal angels are often the special messengers, as they have been in these many stories, sent to help us accept the mysteries that surround us.

These animal angels are testaments to the hope, love and happiness that all humankind can share if we open our hearts and minds to the special bond we share with all other creatures and the life lessons animals can provide. That is the message of this book.